SHAPER

UNLOCK THE POWER OF
MENTAL PERFORMANCE

Copyright © 2022 B. Tom Hunsaker

All rights reserved
Printed in the United States of America FIRST EDITION

No part of this publication may be reproduced, stored in or introduced into a retrieval system, or transmitted, in any form, or by any means (electronic, mechanical, photocopying, recording, or otherwise), without the prior permission of the authors and publisher. Requests for permission should be directed to info@qualtisgroup.com.

Shaper: Unlock the Power of Mental Performance
/Premier Development Edition/B. Tom Hunsaker.

978-0-9985186-5-7

1. Leadership.   2. Strategy.   3. Organizational Culture.
4. Change and Transformation.   5. Management.

Cataloging-in-Publication Data for his book can be obtained from Library of Congress

1 2 3 4 5 6 7 8 9 0

SHAPER

PREMIER DEVELOPMENT EDITION

B. TOM HUNSAKER, PhD

CONTENTS

Preface	vii
Acknowledgements	ix
Chapter 1. The Power of Mindset	1
Chapter 2. Begin Within	19
Chapter 3. Better is the Aim	33
Chapter 4. The Shaper Cycle	51
Chapter 5. Three Levels of Engagement	73
Chapter 6. Cross the Expectation Gap	93
Chapter 7. Two Feet	115
Chapter 8. Build Congruence	149
Chapter 9. Reinforce Your Agency	175
Chapter 10. Provide Effective Feedback	195
Chapter 11. Maximizing Mechanisms	219
Notes	241
About the Author	249

PREFACE

Most worthwhile responses begin with a great question. A question that builds curiosity and doesn't pre-suppose the answer.

Why don't similarly talented people doing similar activities get the same results?

This one question has sweeping implications.

Genetics only tell part of the performance story. And they can't describe rapid and sustained transformations when a person moves from marginal to exceptional results within similar situations.

This work fills this explanation gap. To do so it draws on extensive neuro and social science research, primary interviews and observation on four continents, and grounded case narratives, and applied experience.

It also aspires to something more. Descriptions of phenomena are valuable, but they can frustrate when they're not actionable.

The words *Premier Development Edition* are used to reinforce the pragmatism and applied intentions that guided this book's development — including workshop exercises, thought-provoking prompts, and action opportunities after each chapter to bring the content's principles to life in meaningful, personalized ways.

The goal is that this edition is approachable and aspirational — like it's written with you in mind and provides a compelling spark for what to do next (regardless of your starting point) that can be brought to life through self-guided or workshop-styled engagement.

Ultimately, the value of something is found in its doing. All the best as you embrace the invitation to be a shaper for good — and help others to do the same.

ACKNOWLEDGEMENTS

As the effort of writing this manuscript gave way to reflecting on its process, a deep sense of gratitude to all involved set in.

Saying "by" a single author's name seems inadequate to convey the many whose experiences, discussions, original research, or study participation influenced this effort. Thousands of names contributed to this work — actively and unknowingly. While it is impossible to list them all, there are several groups and individuals I do wish to acknowledge separately. Lasting concepts are rooted in applied experience. Exhaustive study of exceptional performer through the centuries — men and women who dared to stretch the boundaries of what was then common — took me into many workshops, offices, fields and arenas across the globe (some literally, others figuratively). More importantly, I was invited into their patterns of thought to trace commonalities. Thank you for standing apart and for caring enough to document your journeys.

Winston Churchill was fond of saying, "I am always ready to learn, although I do not always like being taught." To the many students in my classes through the years I thank you for being ready to learn and willing to be taught. You have been curious, thoughtful, and insightful. Most importantly, you've shown the value of being 'interested.'

To the many who provided a living laboratory to observe behaviors and validate ideas — thank you for trusting this work's process before it was fully formed and for dedicating countless hours to its refinement. You readily applied concepts in your work, your families, and your relationships and then had the audacity to share what you experienced. This effort would not have been possible without your contribution.

This work was presented in many formats before taking the shape of a book. Thank you to all those who contributed their comments and experiences. Your successes and encouragement provided a deep reservoir to draw from when words didn't want to flow.

It is not uncommon for manuscripts of this nature to linger in a complex state without skilled editorial support. I'm grateful to those who spent many hours helping to shape this work into its present form.

This journey has dotted the globe. Along the way, the best of humanity has been on display. Often in simple ways. CEOs and other executives, public officials, and academics unveiled their lives in intimate ways. Rural villagers welcomed an otherwise stranger, budding entrepreneurs actively embraced probing questions, and many more from a variety of backgrounds welcomed the study of their highs and lows in search of useful trends. The underlying principles and narrative, field tools, use cases, and discovery exercises benefited greatly from your input. Please know that elements of your voice richly informed this work.

Shaper: Premier Development Edition also benefited from discussions with close friends whose feedback is greatly appreciated.

It is said that no one can sustain anything worthwhile without the support of a true confidant. Thank you to a family that endured many late night conversations, wore many hats to support this effort, and for the steady belief in this message and its messenger. Above all, thank you to all who embrace and embody what it means to be a *Shaper*.

PREMIER DEVELOPMENT EDITION

The Premier Development series brings to life leading-edge methods and resources, applied the world over, to help you foster exceptional and sustainable growth.

CHAPTER 1

THE **POWER** OF **MINDSET**

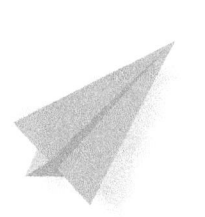

Situated along the Ecuadorian border is a beautiful region home to several small cities and many more towns and villages. The area is rich in natural resources, but for generations it has been poor in most other modern amenities.

Near the turn of the 21st century, mayors from the region's neighboring districts gathered to discuss their situation. The previous decade's technological and economic advancement that flooded other parts of the country had only mildly touched this region. Abutting some of the world's richest waters, the area accounts for nearly 40% of the country's fish exports while employing severely outdated technologies and strategies. Local landowners harvested more mangos than nearly any region in the world, yet they struggle to pay or earn attractive wages; the average family earns less than $10 a day. For as long as locals remember they have lived mainly off of their backs — thinking little more was possible.

Though physically similar to his peers, one mayor stands out from the group. Soft spoken yet assertive, he'd lived his entire life in the same town situated about an hour from the region's largest city. His ancestral identity is linked to this land. But unlike his predecessors, he had the audacity to consider an alternative path for his community — and the willingness to help carve it.

His first step was to enlist the support of neighboring community leaders. For too long, he argued, they had competed with each other for the same subsistence outcomes while the rest of the world passed them by. His message resonated, and soon neighboring mayors were adopting a similar outlook.

Then they did something radical.

They had the idea to have an idea. They shed the near crippling weight of history and circumstance and social forces to imagine what life could become if they enlist their minds as diligently as their backs.

A cooperative among the various communities was formed. They branded themselves as a living economic development laboratory —

agile, responsive, and motivated. They pooled their collective resources to court leading global experts and sold them on the idea that their efforts were best spent in their rural communities — at a fraction of their going rate. Determined ambition replaced thoughts of subsistence. The area began to attract economic development specialists, foreign investment, and higher-value local entrepreneurship. These mayors had re-wired their mindset and, they expected, the future of their people.

The late Steve Jobs, one of the most revered leaders of his time, had a similar experience when in 1996 he returned to guide Apple after unceremoniously resigning from the company he founded over a decade earlier. By his own account he was different – better - when he returned to Apple (which was critical because the company was sputtering prior to his return). He had adopted important lessons during his time away from the company that would shape the firm's future.

While Jobs is best known for the household items Apple would produce (the iPod, iPad, iTunes, and iPhone among others) during his second tenure with the firm, his most important idea wasn't a product or service. His 'do-over' was grounded in something much more abiding than a business model or distribution channel.

It was an approach to work — a new mental pact.

The new mental agreement of Apple didn't have a name, but those around Jobs felt it. Exceptionalism would drive everything in the firm's crusade against simplistic, uninspired products and bulky software that pandered to short-sighted profit calculations.[1] "We try to use the talents we have to express our deep feelings, to show our appreciation of the contributions that came before us, and to add something to the flow," is how Jobs described what would drive the firm going forward.[2]

To Jobs, Apple 2.0 wasn't a product or service. It was a concept, an ideal. Like a lyric that transcends space and time, it was a vehicle to allow

---

1. Mui, C. (2001, November 15). Innovators Beware: The Danger of Viewing Steve Jobs as a 'Tweaker'. Forbes.com.
2. Isaacson, W. (2011) Steve Jobs, Simon & Schuster, pp. 567 — 570.

people to express their best work. Jobs tapped a mentality that shattered previous assumptions of what was possible. And he invited others to do the same.

THE SHAPER EFFECT

As the 2020s approached, scholars at an elite American graduate school began an experiment to understand why people interpret the same events so differently. Nearly 1,000 participants were equally divided into two groups. Both groups were shown the same video of department-store shoppers in everyday situations and asked to independently document what they saw. Neither group was told what to look for, but the second group was given the simple prompt to consider customer frustration.

The study was designed to test two assumptions. The first assumed that responses would vary greatly within each group. People experience the world so differently, the researchers hypothesized, that descriptions of the events from viewing the videos would be more unique than similar. They also wanted to see if the prompt for the second group to consider customer frustration would be heeded even though it lacked specific instructions.

What they found differed wildly from what they expected. Responses varied little within each group — among peer groups they were strikingly similar. Descriptions from group one largely focused on surface events depicted in the video — shoppers' appearance, the store's lighting, lists of products on the shelves– with little regard for the human experiences unfolding within the video. Participants related superficial facts as if they had just finished watching a movie they didn't care about.

Descriptions from group two were much richer, as if they had been given permission to think differently than the other group. The researchers were surprised by the empathy, human interest, and solutions orientation in their comments. Cosmetic observations with little meaning were replaced by considerations of how shoppers felt while engaging their activities. Participants noticed when shoppers couldn't find what they looked for, when an item seemed too far out of the reach of many of the shoppers, or when the store layout created too much work for shoppers wanting an in-and-out experience.

It was as if the two groups had watched completely different videos. Why did a simple, vague prompt cause people to experience their world so differently?

About the same time management researchers were trying to understand why businesses in the same industries with similar resources (managerial talent, product mixes, access to information, capital, and operating environments) have such dramatically different outcomes over time. Filtering through thousands of firms they isolated industry groups of similarly sized, aged, and resourced companies and analyzed them over a seven-year period. Plotting them on a graph with each dot representing a company's starting performance output, the initial diagram for each industry made a relatively tight cluster. After seven years, however, the performance diagram looked very different. Some firms performed exceptionally well — others poorly. Expert strategists, the researchers wanted to describe the difference as brilliant strategic modeling and execution — a stroke of planning genius. But they couldn't.

Reviewing the companies' business plans, operating structures, and business processes provided more questions than answers. The systems, structures, and operating activities of the winners and the losers looked almost identical. The firms had followed similar business models and their business plans read as if they were created in the same room.

So, what explains their different outcomes?

It was only when researchers looked at the behaviors of people within the organizations, rather than the organizations themselves, that they started to understand the difference.

ACTIVITY DISPARITY

Activity dissonance (engaging an activity with one expectation and experiencing another) is a common occurrence and shares roots with cognitive dissonance (discomfort from holding two or more contradictory ideas). Until recently, however, more was known about what it is than how to solve for it. The example of Michael could be any one of thousands of people observed through the course of this work and shows how activity dissonance works.

In his thirties and married with children, Andy's career with a Fortune 500 financial services firm was in jeopardy because he wasn't meeting his goals. He was frustrated. Despite doing more than what his job description and the firm's training program prescribed, his efforts didn't translate into success.

Michael's approach to his lack of success was to work even harder. During a first meeting with Michael he described his goals. As an advisor whose primary job is to cultivate new clients and manage their investment portfolio, he said it was to make 33 contacts a day. Pressed to describe why that was his goal he said that because the company told him to make 25 contacts a day, and 33 is more than 25, by making more contacts he would be more successful than the average employee.

"Are you?"
"Am I what?"
"Successful."
"I think so, yes."
"Then why do your outcomes say differently?"

Andy had succumbed to the common misconception that completing tasks related to a desired result will necessarily bring about that result. When this doesn't happen an expectation gap forms that's difficult to reconcile. This author has observed a similar effect in roles as researcher, professor, and business leader in nearly two dozen countries. In each case, when the anticipated corollary (outcomes equal to input efforts) doesn't materialize, confusion and frustration follow.

After a few moments of silence Andy responded.

"I'm here because I'm not making any money."
"Is your goal to make money or to make contacts?"

Silence.

Breaking the long pause, "It can't be both. One is an activity and one is a goal."

He clarified that his goal is to make money and his activity is to make contacts. Asking why he isn't making money by making so many contacts naturally followed.

"That's what I don't get."

A dynamic conversation followed regarding what he thinks about when he's making these contacts.

"I focus on getting their phone number so I can call them later with a good investment idea."
"When you call them later how do they react?"
"They never buy."

Andy wanted to do a good job. Work ethic couldn't explain his lack of success — he worked harder than many others at his firm. His social skills were serviceable, his intellect above average, and his personal integrity and interest in others was easily detected within a few minutes of talking with him — so genetic disadvantage or an inability to build trust weren't the issue.

Andy then accepted the invitation to take a different approach for the next month.

Rather than focusing on the number of contacts to be made, his job was to focus on what was personally meaningful to him in making contacts and to consider the same in those he would contact. We provided him with specific tools to help along the way and agreed to meet again at the end of the month.

The last Friday of that month Andy had different news to share. He had just finished the most productive period in his financial services career. Not once did he make 33 contacts in a day, but by the end of the month he had secured nearly two million dollars in new business — while working the same area he'd already been through dozens of times.

> "Before making contacts I would think about the people I was about to meet. I focused on how much I enjoy being around people and envisioned meeting people who had enough money for me to provide well for my family. I thought of how these people needed my help. I thought of doing incredibly well by them and being their financial partner for the rest of their lives — and how I would treat them if I knew we'd have a relationship for that long. I experienced a shift."

What Andy had discovered and research supports is that one's capacity to influence personal outcomes is remarkably pliable.[3][4][5] While genetics and environment have an impact, managing how you perceive your actions more directly determines your chances of success.

IT'S THEIR HEAD

"Veteran. Worked my whole life. Please help — God bless." The words were neatly written in black ink on a small brown poster. The man holding the sign appeared to be in his sixties. He was groomed as well as could be expected in the warm Phoenix sun. His face was tanned from the direct heat and wore an expression somewhere between resiliency and defeat. He didn't want to be in that situation and appeared to be genuinely in need.

He had positioned himself on the median near the stop light for the left-hand turning lane. It is commonly accepted that less than 20% of people

---

[3] Huntsinger, J. R., Isbell, L. M., & Clore, G. L. (2014). The affective control of thought: Malleable, not fixed. Psychological review, 121(4), 600.

[4] Taylor, S. E., & Gollwitzer, P. M. (1995). Effects of mindset on positive illusions. Journal of personality and social psychology, 69(2), 213.

[5] Fiske, S. T., & Taylor, S. E. (2013). Social cognition: From brains to culture. Sage.

worldwide give to others asking for money in the street—for a number of reasons. This scene was no different. Each time the light turned red, drivers in the line of cars avoided making eye contact with the man. Instead, they fidgeted with the radio or other items on the dashboard, turned to talk to a passenger in the car, or simply starred at the stoplight ahead.

The man smiled and waved as each car passed by him.

What happened next is similar to the experience a group of friends had while camping in the Rocky Mountains.

A man we'll call Tim, one of the members of the group and an expert horseman, brought horses for whomever wanted to ride. One of Tim's friends, despite having limited experience, was eager to give riding a try. So, they made plans to wake up early the next morning and test a trail they had scouted earlier in the day.

Tim rode a tall quarter horse and saddled his friend on a deep black Arabian. They started on the trail slowly. Along the way Tim gave his friend some tips. The most important thing he shared was, "Never give the horse his head."

About a quarter mile into the trail the riders came to a gravel road. Tim's friend saw his opportunity to test his new riding skills and dug his heels in to the horse to see what it could do. The horse launched forward.

As the road turned to a sharp corner Tim's friend could feel the horse's feet slipping from underneath him. Just before losing its footing, the horse was able to gain composure and stay upright. Watching the scene unfold, Tim dug into his horse to catch up to his friend, panting nearly as heavily as the horse that carried him there as he chided,

"Never do that."

The rest of the trail ride was uneventful until Tim and his friend approached their base camp. To get there, they had to cross a large meadow — the kind from a John Wayne movie with mountains in every direction and pine trees framing the edges of tall green grass.

Tim's friend asked if he could take the horse for a short run through the meadow. As he did, he dug in his heels and let the horse hit stride. The horse started going so fast that Tim's friend had to squeeze his legs as tight as he could around the horse's belly to try to stay on as it continued to pick up pace. He tried to pull back on the reins. Nothing. Finally, he reached as far up to the horse's face as he could and pulled the reins down until the horse's face was tucked against his right shoulder. The horse finally submitted and slowed to a stop.

Worried and upset, Tim again rode up to his friend and yelled,

"I told you to never give him his head."

The friend explained that he didn't know what that meant.

"This horse is incredibly powerful. Giving him his head means you allow enough slack in the reins for him to feel like he controls his destiny. Once he gets that in his mind, there's no stopping him."

The scene of that military veteran on the street asking for help, and the extraordinary turn of events that followed, shows what can happen when we give people their heads.

As the next red light came, the man assumed his familiar position. He had come to expect a conscious avoidance from passersby, so he almost didn't believe when someone in a modest sedan waived for him to come closer. At first, he hesitated and then he cautiously shuffled to the car.

The driver did more than give the man money. He rolled down his window and engaged him. We don't know what was said, but they talked for about 30 seconds. When they finished their conversation, the driver looked the man in the eyes and reached out to shake his hand. Both nodded to each other in affirmation. Then the driver in the next car did the same thing. And the driver behind her. Then the driver behind him. Others in the line saw what was happening and soon they, too, volunteered of themselves to this man. A spontaneous movement had formed where just two minutes earlier the man stood at the same street corner, dejected, as a line of cars ignored him.

Statistics show that few, if any, in the line intended to help that man prior to watching someone else take the initiative.[6][7][8] But in an instant, they changed their minds. And this new thought radically changed their actions. To be sure, the humanizing effect of seeing another reach out his hand to validate this man had an impact. But there is something more to this pattern — something fundamental to success that can be learned and repeated.

For premier leaders, it begins by considering what happens when people are given their heads.

---

6   Janis, I. L. (2008). Groupthink. IEEE Engineering Management Review, 36(1), 36.
7   Heckhausen, J., & Heckhausen, H. (Eds.). (2008). Motivation and action (Vol. 22). New York: Cambridge University Press.
8   Clark, R. D., & Word, L. E. (1972). Why don't bystanders help? Because of ambiguity?. Journal of Personality andSocial Psychology, 24(3), 392.

DISCOVERY SECTION

PART I: RESPOND

Respond to the questions below using the following rating scale:

A = Always. B = Often. C = Sometimes. D = Rarely. E = Never.

1. When trying to improve results from an activity do you first focus on doing more of it? ☐

2. How often do you take decisions that are different than what others are doing? ☐

3. Do you daily think about what you think about? ☐

PART II: DESCRIBE

For the following questions, describe how you would most likely respond. To get the most from your efforts, don't describe what you think you should do, but rather what you would most likely do based on how you've responded to similar situations in the past.

You engage in an activity and don't get the desired result. How would you likely mentally respond in this situation?

_____
_____
_____
_____
_____
_____
_____
_____

DISCOVERY SECTION

You are under a deadline and know that your work will not likely be checked — as long as it's delivered on time. What commitment to quality will you likely show in this situation?

DISCOVERY SECTION

PRACTICE ACTIVITIES SECTION

Compare two scenarios from your recent experiences — one more and one less successful. What did you think about prior to the outcome?

How did your mindset possibly influence the result?

- Experience #1 — More Successful

- Experience #2 — Less Successful

DISCOVERY SECTION

Given a similar scenario going forward, how could you build from the more successful elements and improve on the less successful ones?

DISCOVERY SECTION

Generally, what thought patterns can you identify for when you're most hopeful? When you're most fearful?

CHAPTER 2

BEGIN **WITHIN**

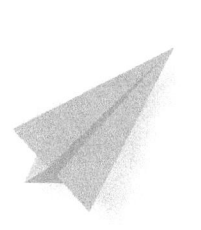

It was like watching someone unwrap a thoughtful gift. The first thing that caught the attention of the group of art critics, beyond the normal commentary of her eyes, was the softness of her hands.

The Louvre museum in Paris is home to one of the premier art collections in the world. Among the more famous items is the Mona Lisa. Each year millions make their way through the gallery's crowded halls to view Da Vinci's masterpiece.

Few will argue that the Mona Lisa isn't aesthetically stunning. But a small minority understand that more than a surface glance is needed to unlock her true genius. With this work, Da Vinci seemed intent to produce more than just a painting. The subtle sfumato technique he pioneered simultaneously brightens and softens sharp edges through a series of tiny, determined brush strokes.

The detailed layering of paint to canvas (one on top of the other patiently applied over time) gives a chameleon-like characteristic to the work that allows each observer to personalize her to taste. These techniques themselves are their own masterpiece.

It's not by accident that she's the most famous face in the world. She was designed to be.

She's also among the most copied.

Even Da Vinci's own students tried to replicate his masterpiece. But they couldn't. And despite countless attempts, no one since that time has been able to, either. Her genius is found, at least in part, in her originality.

It's as if Da Vinci was nudging others to consider the process for creating something exceptional — and finding one's voice in that effort.

COPIES

The 1960's and 1970's was a furious period for social science and management research. Societal differences ran deep, and scholars committed to developing theories to explain those differences. The business sector was particularly interested in what they had to say. A virtuous cycle formed; organizations wanted to accelerate growth and researchers advocated various differentiation strategies they thought would help organizations achieve that goal. The marketplace couldn't get enough of these new insights.

Near the end of that period, two little known sociologists stepped back from the popular trend of studying differences and asked what would become pivotal to understanding of how many organizations function. As if they had discovered a typo in an important manuscript, they noticed that reality didn't completely match theory. Despite catchy phrases to the contrary, most organizations acted far more like each other than different.

So, they asked a counter question. What if, instead, they studied why organizations are so similar?

What emerged was the explanation of powerful forces that can prompt organizations to morph into firms similar to theirs — uncovering why input activities tend to be so similar across organizations.

They called it *mimetic isomorphism*.[9]

Leaning on Max Weber's classical analogy of the iron cage, mimetic isomorphism highlights the tendency of an organization to imitate how another organization operates because it believes that there are benefits to doing so.[10] For example, if the logos were removed from all airports, airplanes, and employees it would be difficult to distinguish one airline company from another — but for a few cases. The same can be said for banks or any other number of industries.

The thinking is that mirroring the behaviors of others provides legitimacy

---

9   DiMaggio, P., & Powell, W. W. (1983). The iron cage revisited: Collective rationality and institutional isomorphism in organizational fields. American Sociological Review, 48(2), 147-60.

10 Weber, M. (1946 [1922]). Class, status, party. In Gerth, H.H. and Wright Mills, C.(Eds). From Max Weber essays in sociology (180-195). New York: Oxford University Press, pp. 180-195.

or a sense of belonging – believing there is safety in the crowd. Like living on borrowed reputation, the reason to mimic others is the desire to be perceived as more similar to those who are revered.

Dozens, then hundreds of examples poured in of organizations trying to describe themselves as unique, but whose distinctions were more superficial than substantial. They were better described as a copy of a copy. More directly, though their input activities closely mirrored others in their industry their outcomes varied. Tens of thousands of scholarly citations and as many actual cases support that this phenomenon is every bit as prevalent today.

While some protection can be found in mimicry, there are also tremendous costs. Consider any of the great innovations in modern history. Not one of them would have occurred without the conscious effort to break from the social forces of imitation.

Southwest would not have reimagined what is possible in the airline industry. Apple would not have redefined the personal computing, music, and telecommunications spaces. No Google. No Amazon. No Starbucks. If unchecked, mimicry suppresses the instinct to develop original thoughts and work.

Despite advances in technology, each time a photocopy is made it becomes further removed from the original document. Eventually, a copy of a copy can become unintelligible — regardless of the photocopy maker's strong desires to be viewed in the same light as the original. Not to be confused with modeling (learning from or personalizing certain behavioral cues that are relevant to one's experience), an imitation is inferior by definition. Because a copy is never as potent as the original, those who fall prey to this thinking artificially cap their potential — hindering their capacity to learn, adapt, and grow.

The irony to mimicry is that copying others' activities alone rarely produces the same outcome.

While *mimetic isomorphism* and related work were designed to describe organizations, you can see how this concept is also relevant to individuals.[11] [12] [13] [14] [15]

PEOPLE IMITATIONS

Susan is the kind of professional others want to emulate.[16] Engaging, hardworking, dependable, and successful it's not surprising that her firm tried to replicate his performance by having her train nearly a dozen salespeople over a two-year period. What did surprise the firm was that not one of her trainees became equally successful.

Susan's approach is to understand the controllable activities the firm requires and then to do more of them. For example, if twenty phone calls are asked of the employee Susan doubles that number and does forty. If the prescription is to daily go door-to-door for an hour seeking out clients in the community — Susan goes out for two hours. With each encounter Susan's goal is to introduce herself, leave a business card, and then call that person consistently for the next two months.

This process brought Susan a lot of success. The firm knew of Susan's approach and appreciated that she followed metrics they thought could be easily tracked and would translate well to others. Trusting her recipe, they expected that Susan's discipline and consistency would turn out success stories like her own.

To Susan's credit, she was a model trainer. She did exactly what she said

---

11 Singelis, T. M. (1994). The measurement of independent and interdependent self construals. Personality and Social Psychology Bulletin, 20(5), 580-591.
12 Lee, K., & Pennings, J. M. (2002). Mimicry and the market: Adoption of a new organizational form. Academy of Management Journal, 45(1), 144-162.
13 Grey, C. (2004). 'Reinventing business schools: the contribution of critical management education', Academy of Management Learning and Education, 3, pp. 178–186.
14 Kim, W. C., & Mauborgne, R. (2004). Blue ocean strategy. If you read nothing else on strategy, read these best-selling articles., 71.
15 Wilson, D., & McKiernan, P. (2011). Global mimicry: Putting strategic choice back on the business school agenda. British Journal of Management, 22(3), 457-469.
16 Susan is a pseudonym to protect the participant's identity

she would do, and she patterned precisely the behaviors for her trainees to follow. She was encouraging when needed and tough when required. She followed up with her trainees and held them accountable to the formula she had prescribed. And they closely followed what she told them to do.

Most failed and left the company or performed below the firm average for that position.

Talking with Susan about her training approach, she had few answers for the lack of success. Neither did the firm. The recipe of disciplined effort, pushing beyond activity requirements, and consistent accountability seemed like a winning formula. On the surface it is.

Beneath the surface is something more profound.

Without contextual effectiveness and personal relevance, the copy struggles to replicate the intent of an activity — it only mirrors its motions.

When trainees had challenges, bad days, or wanted to interject new ideas, Susan thought she would save them the trouble of thinking too much. She reasoned that the formula had already been created and they just needed to follow it. Like an assembly plant for human behavior, Susan's standard phrase was "don't think about it — just work the plan."

By trying to bypass the thought process, however, she stripped out a key factor to outcomes success — effectively managing one's mindset (thoughts or intentions).[17][18]

Think of a well-made, but fake currency. It can fool the passive observer for a time, but it will never fully satisfy the intent of the original: to provide its owner with equivalent purchasing power. What was profound and relevant to Susan because she had made the approach her own was

---

17 "Mind–set." Merriam-Webster.com. Merriam-Webster, n.d. Web. August 1, 2015.
18 Dweck, C.S. (2006). Mindset: The new psychology of success. New York, NY, US: Random House.

simply a list of rules to follow and tasks to complete to those who tried to copy her.[19]

Because others hadn't invested in making the process personally meaningful, they developed a twisted mental concept for success — completing a list of tasks. This was evident when Susan's trainees interacted with prospective clients. Rather than conveying genuine interest in others, they were calculated and robotic. And the outcome they hoped for never came. Whether they made twenty calls or forty calls was irrelevant because their mindset when engaging the activity was counterfeit.

AGENTS ON ENVIRONMENTS

A distinct British accent comes through as the reporter leans forward and asks a young girl, "Who would you want to be like?"

The story is set in the backstreets of Compton, California, known globally for its social challenges. Compton's poverty rate has historically been among the highest in America.[20] Poverty and violent crime rates are not far behind. During the decade in which this young girl grew up, a resident of Compton was over ten times more likely to be murdered than those from neighboring cities in southern California.

The first thing that surprised the reporter is the young girl's sport of choice. There is little about Compton's environment that would prompt a child to play tennis. Few public courts exist, and those that do are worn (mainly from neglect). It's not a common sport among school-aged children so there are few social reasons to take it up.

Yet day after day this young girl worked at her craft along with her sister and father. She would become one of the world's greatest players of the sport.

---

19 Frankl, V.E. (2006). Man's search for meaning. Boston: Beacon Press.
20 http://quickfacts.census.gov/qfd/states/06/0615044.html. Retrieved December 30, 2015.

Serena Williams is a naturally gifted athlete. But so are thousands of other children in any city around the world.

What makes her unique was foreshadowed many years before she first took the court for a professional tournament when that reporter asked her as a young girl who she wanted to be like.

"Well, I'd like other people to be like me."[21]

The young Serena's wry smile and direct eye contact as she said those words hinted that she really believed them. Her astounding success over two decades as a tennis professional are the evidence.

At a very young age she understood something that eludes most. Mindset is among the most powerful ways to determine outcomes. This is where success begins — and ends. And a mindset can be shaped or positioned independent of the environment in which it resides.

The common path is to use social benchmarking to determine what is possible (framing your potential by comparing yourself to your surroundings). More than seeking reference points to make sense of the world around you, this form of benchmarking passively outsources to the social environment one's future prospects. Think of an airplane that is operating on autopilot. Rather than intentionally charting its course, it floats through the air in a subconscious-like state — waiting for someone to provide the next set of directions.[22]

In the common path your best prospect is to become the *average* of the environment in which you reside.

To anyone who has walked the hallways of a high school in any number of countries or observed meeting interactions in randomly selected companies this is clear.

---

21 https://www.youtube.com/watch?v=3K_4LfzKPko. Retrieved November 23, 2015.
22 Singelis, T. M. (1994). The measurement of independent and interdependent self-construals. Personality and Social Psychology Bulletin, 20(5), 580-591.

The other path is to consciously engage your mindset as you chart intentional decisions. Different from a personality trait, which is described as inherent or fixed,[23] one's mindset is surprisingly malleable.[24] And the process to effectively shape one's mindset is inclusive (nearly anyone can do it) and straightforward (it does not require a lot of time or technical skill). Perhaps most important, doing so doesn't necessarily depend upon changing one's surroundings or the participants in it.

Grounded in primary studies, experiences, and pivotal work from neuro and the social sciences, the case for effective Shaper is compelling. Research shows that performance in nearly every metric — creativity, engagement, productivity, fulfillment — improves when certain approaches to shape one's mindset are employed.

Just as software depends on the quality of input information to succeed or fail in its job, based on the direction it receives one's mindset is incredibly adept at facilitating or sabotaging desired interests. Knowing how to identify and affect that process (and to teach others to do the same) fundamentally impacts most conceivable quality measures.

The remaining chapters provide applied frameworks, use cases, and practical methods for recognizing and effectively shape one's mindset in any situation.

---

23 Bouchard, T. J. and McGue, M. (2003), Genetic and environmental influences on human psychological differences. J. Neurobiol., 54: 4–45. doi: 10.1002/ neu.10160
24 Yeager, D. S. & Dweck, C. S. (2012). Mindsets That Promote Resilience: When Students Believe That Personal Characteristics Can Be Developed. Educational Psychologist, 47(4), 302–314, 2012.

PART I: RESPOND

Respond to the questions below using the following rating scale:

A = Always. B = Often. C = Sometimes. D = Rarely. E = Never.

4. How often is your dominant motive to fit in with your surroundings?
5. How often is your dominant motive to shape your surroundings?
6. When interacting with others, how often do you suggest that they simply follow the formula instead of thinking for themselves?

PART II: DESCRIBE

For the following questions, describe how you would most likely respond. To get the most from your efforts, don't describe what you think you should do, but rather what you would most likely do based on how you've responded to similar situations in the past.

You see the opportunity to mimic someone's efforts — hoping to gain a short cut to success. How would you likely respond in this situation?

_____

_____

_____

Consider the statement "The common path is to use social benchmarking to determine what is possible (framing your potential by comparing yourself to your surroundings)" and outline whether and how this describes your current approach.

_____

_____

DISCOVERY SECTION

PRACTICE ACTIVITIES SECTION

Compare two scenarios from your recent experiences — one more and one less successful. How did your surroundings determine your actions? How did you determine to shape your surroundings?

- Experience #1 — More Successful

- Experience #2 — Less Successful

DISCOVERY SECTION

Given a similar scenario going forward, how could you build from the more successful elements and improve on the less successful ones?

DISCOVERY SECTION

Generally, what patterns can you identify when you're likely to allow your surroundings to drive your mindset? When you determine to shape your surroundings?

CHAPTER 3

BETTER IS THE **AIM**

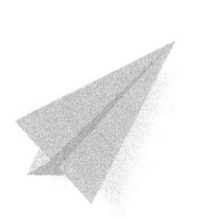

This and related work have involved interviewing CEOs and executives in multinational companies across the world about their biggest challenges. One experience highlights a common thought pattern. Charles[25] works in business development for General Motors (GM). When we met, he expressed deep frustration with what he thought was a lack of engagement from his people.

"If we could get our people to do more, we would be that much better off."

That sentiment was shared by an executive director of internal sales for another Fortune 500 company. To get his teams more involved and to raise their proficiency, he requires them to participate in daily trainings. At a group dinner we sat with one of the team members and asked what he thought of the heavy training requirement.

Well-educated and socially skilled, he expressed appreciation that the trainings helped him to be a better resource for his clients.

We probed deeper. "Do the more veteran people resent the training since they've already learned so much?"

"No, I think it still helps them to be a better client resource."
"Why do you personally feel the training is important?"

Up to that point we had been given answers that read like a company brochure. They were the words he was supposed to say, but they didn't seem to be the words he really believed.

"Honestly, I do it because it's required and because I don't want to look stupid in front of my clients."

Born of fear, completing a task to not look incompetent is a different motivation than wanting to personally develop and to improve others.

"What do you think about when you're doing the trainings?"

---

25 Charles is a pseudonym to protect the participant's identity.

"I really just focus on getting through them in the time given me. Then I write down a tip or two and try to implement them with my clients that day."

"Off the top of your head, how many tips that you've written down can you remember?"

Silence — interrupted only by awkward non-verbal expressions that come with not knowing how to answer a question. Completing the daily trainings had done little to influence the way he approached his work.[26]

These examples are not the exception. In one of the largest studies of its kind involving 25,000 executives and managers (part of a four-decade undertaking including 2.5 million manager-led teams), Gallup found that 70% feel disengaged from their work. That number increases to 83% worldwide. A natural consequence of disengagement is underperformance. Leaders sense this untapped potential and instinctively want to fill it by assigning or requiring more because quantity of effort is straightforward to control.

The problem is that doing more itself doesn't correlate to better results. Commonly, success and failure share similar activities that have been undertaken through different mental lenses. It's rarely what's done, alone, that makes the difference — but rather, how it's done.

Like a self-fulfilling prophecy, the cycle of prescribing more activities, more time, and more urgent effort to drive performance and emphasizing what to do — over why it should be done — can actually deepen disengagement (emotional detachment), resentment (perceived unfair treatment), and misunderstanding (failure to connect). Busy is not the same as productive. And more is not the same as better.

This disconnect is rooted in how our brains work. While incredibly powerful, the brain struggles to be in two places at one time. When anxiety levels increase, the amygdala activates (the part of the brain that

---

26   Beck, R. and Harter, J. (2015). Managers Account for 70% of Variance in Employee Engagement. Gallup Business Journal. Retrieved July 8, 2015.

detects and responds to threats) — which hinders the prefrontal cortex (the part of the brain responsible for effective problem solving) from doing its job.[27] [28] [29] [30] Unmet, unfounded, or misunderstood demands are leading culprits of heightened anxiety.

Without sharpening the mental lens of why and how people find meaning in their activities, it's unlikely that doing them more frequently will have the intended effect.

THE VALUE OF MEANINGFUL

Working with a prominent healthcare company, participants were asked to write down a personal or business activity that they feel is important. Asked to share, one woman in attendance offered that an important personal activity to her is to monitor her son's daily electronic usage. *I will monitor my son's electronic usage* went on the white board in the room followed by the word *because*.

Since actions are just empty movements until they're assigned purpose, this woman was asked her why that was an important activity to her. "That's my job as a parent."

"How often do you monitor your son's electronic activity?"
"Not as often as I should"

Her words were laced with guilt. Important enough to be one of the first things that came to her mind, this activity hadn't yet converted to consistent, self-driven behavior. Being important wasn't enough to drive her to action. And when she did act, she didn't get the reaction she wanted from her son.

---

27 LeDoux, J. E. (2014). Coming to terms with fear. Proceedings of the National Academy of Sciences, 111(8), 2871-2878.
28 Lieberman, M. D. (2007). Social cognitive neuroscience: a review of core processes. Annu. Rev. Psychol., 58, 259-289.
29 Davidson, R. J. (2002). Anxiety and affective style: role of prefrontal cortex and amygdala. Biological psychiatry, 51(1), 68-80.
30 Fiske, S. T., & Taylor, S. E. (2013). Social cognition: From brains to culture. Sage. 152-171.

"Talk about the quality of your interactions with your son when you do 'monitor' him."

"Not very good."

"What do you mean?"

"He seems to resent me for checking up on him. That frustrates me, and I'm sure that comes across when I interact with him."

This brave volunteer was then asked to flip the order of the words "because" and "I will" and invited to view this activity with different perspective.

Because____ I will____

"Why is it your job as a parent to monitor your son's electronic usage?"

"Because I am his mother and I want him to be productive"

"Why do you care if he is productive" we asked.

"Because I want him to grow up and get a good job and be a good member of the community."

"Why do you care if he is a good member of the community and gets a good job?"

"Because I want him to be happy."

"Why do you want him to be happy?"

"Because I love him."

Something came over her as she started to make the connection.

Because I love my son, I will monitor his electronic usage.

Consider the mental frames in her first two responses: first to simply name a task and then to describe the task through a sense of obligation ("it's my job"). These are themes commonly assigned to activities one believes are important (of consequence), but the *why* hasn't been consciously articulated. Too often importance, by itself, is processed abstractly — unless something else is attached to it. So, filling our heads and others' calendars with piles of important tasks tends to either overwhelm and paralyze effective problem solving or produce disjointed activity commitment — statically pushing a button without considering quality or intention.

Meaningfulness is processed very differently from importance. When something is meaningful — defined here as a positive act that is relevant, worthwhile, and deeply personal — it shifts from an abstract assignment to concrete interest. The focus moves from output to outcome.

Think of concreteness as turning an idea into a real application. For example, saying to someone who is trying to change an eating habit that a certain meal contains 100 grams of fat will have limited meaning. That amount of fat, while it sounds large, is hard to envision and equate to potential impact. Now, take the same meal and state that it is the equivalent of eating a Big Mac from McDonald's and a pan of bacon. In both examples the same information is conveyed, but the second example is more relevant because it can be personally experienced (inviting an intellectual *and* emotional response) — the sight and sound of bacon frying in the pan and the grease residue in the Big Mac packaging trigger sensations that bring to life an otherwise arbitrary number, 100 grams.

Elements of this principle extend from early sociology work in symbolic interactionism. George H. Mead and his protégé Herbert Blumer describe three conditions that influence why people choose to do one thing over another. Most fitting, humans act toward things on the basis of the meanings they ascribe to those things and those meanings are handled in, and modified through, an interpretive process used by the person in dealing with the things he or she encounters.[31] [32] [33] In other words, people seek to do what they find most meaningful — and they signal to others what they find to be most meaningful by what they do.

No one has infinite time or resources. When people are compelled to do more of an activity that might be important, but one that they don't find personally meaningful, frustration sets in. And when they engage other

---

31 Charon, Joel M. (2004). Symbolic Interactionism An Introduction, An Interpretation, An Integration. Boston: Pearson. p.
32 Blumer, H. (1969) Symbolic Interactionism; Perspective and Method. Englewood Cliffs, NJ: Prentice-Hall
33 Mead, G. H. (1934). Mind, self and society (Vol. 111). University of Chicago Press.: Chicago.

activities at the expense of what they profess to be meaningful — for example, watching excessive TV instead of engaging one's children — a sense of guilt tends to follow. Both result in busyness, but not necessarily effectiveness. This author's research has noted time and again how the subtle shift from importance to meaningfulness transforms the way people view otherwise similar events. It is key to infuse essential activities with personal meaning — catalyzing your efforts.

By placing the reason why something is done (*because*) in front of the activity commitment (*I will*), a mental ordering takes place that attaches personal meaning where it might have otherwise been overlooked, muted, or discarded. *You don't have to love the activity — just the reason why you do it.* Then rote motions give way to dynamic purpose. Whereas, muddying this sequence can eave activities feeling arbitrary and contrived, evoking negative emotions and stunting interest.

All meaningful activities are important, but not all-important activities are meaningful.

Meaningfulness is also valuable because it moves beyond simplistic calculations of object rewards or reprimands to tap a deeper well of positive human motivation. For example, a common managerial technique is to have employees think of something they'd really like — a car, a vacation, a phone — and then to put a picture of that item on their desk to motivate extra effort. There is limited research to justify that approach, however, other than a momentary bump in urgency. More often people get energized and then stop at the sign of difficulty — convincing themselves that there are other important things to take its place or that the object they desired really isn't that significant.

Important is rarely enough to sustain effort, while meaningfulness tends to have a multiplier effect — exceeding what was previously considered possible.

Looking beneath the surface, the real *because* isn't a new car; it's the prospect of being viewed positively by others or the envisioned experiences that car represents and the people involved in those experiences. Emerging neuroscience suggests our brains will forget or detach from superfluous (excess) items in order to remain efficient.[34] [35] [36] [37] [38]

When pressed, like one more bite after you've already eaten your fill, even important items can be disregarded if their meaning hasn't been firmly embedded into how you view the task.

How much love that woman in the healthcare company felt for her son didn't change during that five-minute exchange with her. Nor did her feeling that monitoring her son's electronic usage is important. But her capacity to prioritize that love instantly impacted the way she viewed the task. And, in her view, that re-prioritization significantly affects how well she will undertake it going forward.

"Please share with the group how you envision the next electronics monitoring interplay with your son."

By now simplistic responses had turned to rich, thoughtful dialogue. Instead of doing it because it is her 'job,' tears filled her eyes as she warmly expressed how her tone will change going forward. By consciously viewing these exchanges through the meaningful place of loving and wanting the best for her son (putting *because* at the beginning of the action equation), she inserted the missing motivation to an otherwise rote task on a to-do list of many. The activity will be the same, but her approach to it will be significantly better.

---

34 Davis, R. L., & Zhong, Y. (2017). The biology of forgetting—a perspective. Neuron, 95(3), 490-503.

35 Richards, B. A., & Frankland, P. W. (2017). The persistence and transience of memory. Neuron, 94(6), 1071-1084.

36 Sachser, R. M., Haubrich, J., Lunardi, P. S., & de Oliveira Alvares, L. (2017). Forgetting of what was once learned: ExpLizng the role of postsynaptic ionotropic glutamate receptors on memory formation, maintenance, and decay. Neuropharmacology, 112, 94-103.

37 Hadziselimovic, N., Vukojevic, V., Peter, F., Milnik, A., Fastenrath, M., Fenyves, B. G., & Papassotiropoulos, A. (2014). Forgetting is regulated via Musashi-mediated translational control of the Arp2/3 complex. Cell,156(6), 1153-1166.

38 McGaugh, J. L. (2000). Memory--a century of consolidation. Science, 287(5451), 248-251.

She finished by describing that she envisioned her son responding differently because she would engage him from a new mental position. What she previously perceived to be a chore and her son viewed as an attack or condescension could now be seen as a mutual interest to care for and develop her son's potential.

In her words: "It will never be the same."

BECAUSE, I WILL CANVAS

Approach	Observed frequency	Description	Likely outcome
Task statement	Most Common	"_X_ is needed."	Below Average
Task statement with explanation of its importance	Common	"_X_ is needed, because _Y_"	Average
Description of meaningfulness	Least Common	"*Because* _Y_, I will _X_."	Exceptional
In practice (Build your own because I will)		Objective: *Because:* Reason why objective is meaningful *I will:* Action to ensure the meaningful is achieved	

Figure 1

FROM QN TO QL

A sales manager tasked with developing a new area for his firm grew discouraged when success came slowly. To help himself muscle through the day's activities, he created a point system for every contact he made. One point for a call and two points for a face-to-face interaction. He described to us that achieving a certain number of points in the day helped him to feel like it was worth the effort.

You can imagine the results from his scheme. He had engineered a system that rewarded the quantity of his efforts, while numbing him to the effects of their quality. This case may be extreme, but consider how many ways you or people around you design mechanisms to muscle through or increase an activity's quantity without tackling the heart of where the difference really occurs — quality through meaningfulness.

It is helpful to think of a simple equation. X (activity) + Y (quantity) = Z (result). On the surface, it appears the best way to grow the result (Z) is to simply increase (Y).

In practice, the equation's operator and the order of the variables don't stay constant. The addition sign shifts to a division or a multiplication symbol based on the mental approach of the person engaging the equation and the (X) and the (Y) trade places for the same reason.

Think of these as two new equations, QN (Quantity) and QL (Quality). In the QN equation, quantity is top of mind and outweighs concerns for how well something is done — the rationale is doing a lot of something will compensate for any failings in the activity or bypass needing to build meaning into what is done.

The QN equation usually acts this way:

QN 1000 (Y) quantity ÷ 10 (X) activity = 10 (Z) result More resources are spent chasing smaller returns.

The QL equation emphasizes techniques to mentally position people for magnified quality, which better leverages its return on quantity.

QL tends to snowball the favorable impact of activities:
QL 10 (X) activity x 100 (Y) quantity = 1000 (Z) result More is produced from similar or fewer resources.

While quantity and quality aren't mutually exclusive (if one is present the other can't be), their order and emphasis matter because they influence whether a multiplier or division symbol will likely take effect. A mental frame can nullify huge amounts of effort or magnify the same. Quality isn't about doing less. It's about getting more from what is done.

Figure 2 provides a visual representation of the power of quality over mere quantity.

DEPICTION OF EFFECTIVE QL (QUALITY) RELATIVE TO INEFFECTIVE QN (QUANTITY)

Figure 2

SAVING A RECORD

Many will remember the 2008 Beijing summer Olympics for Michael Phelps breaking Mark Spitz's record by winning eight gold medals in a single Olympic Games. Fewer will appreciate the herculean role Jason Lezak played in helping Phelps to break that record.

In world-class sprint swimming, tenths of a second might as well be miles. Anchoring the American 4x100-meter freestyle relay as the oldest member of the team, Lezak began the final leg of the race with what most thought to be an insurmountable deficit. Worse, the French team in the lead was anchored by the 6'5-inch Alain Bernard (the then world record holder in the 100-meter freestyle).

At one point in the last lap of the race, Bernard had nearly a full body length's lead on Lezak. Seeing that and knowing how hard it is to make up even inches in a single lap, the NBC television announcers (Dan Hicks and Rowdy Gaines) began to talk about the French team as the race's foregone winners, "I just don't think he can do it; the United States trying to hang on to second; they should get the silver medal; Australia is in Bronze."

Prior to those Olympics, Lezak made some dramatic changes to how he approached competition. He opted to self-coach — nearly unprecedented in world-class swimming. Lezak cut the number of hours he trained daily by almost half, but focused intensely on listening to his body and customizing a training regimen fit for that time in his career.

And that day in early August of 2008 he shattered the world record for a 100-meter freestyle split by nearly six-tenths of a second, winning the 4x100-meter relay for his team in sensational fashion.[39]

It's tempting to idolize the outcome in Lezak's story, but the real genius is in his process. Like Da Vinci, rather than copying others he was deeply committed to painting his own masterpiece by adapting techniques to his unique strengths — making them meaningful. The goal or task of winning the race was the same, but to hear him speak there was a distinctly agile quality to his training approach. No longer was it about a certain number of hours in the pool. Training became a creative, intentional act.

---

[39] "U.S. men set world record in 400 free relay." NBC News. 10 August 2008. Retrieved August 3, 2015.

To be sure, Lezak got good ideas from others. But more importantly, he harnessed a mental approach that allowed him to personalize a strategy to his situation. While some of his actions might have looked similar to what others do, the investment to make them his own catalyzed his efforts and provided a reservoir of resilience when needed. He successfully sidestepped the trap of reaching for rote solutions to dynamic needs.

In short, Jason Lezak mastered the process treated in detail next–the Shaper cycle.

DISCOVERY SECTION

PART I: RESPOND

Respond to the questions below using the following rating scale:

A = Always. B = Often. C = Sometimes. D = Rarely. E = Never.

7. How often do you prescribe increasing activity quantity when seeking a better result?

8. How often do you start your day with a 'to-do' list of tasks, but not a mental reminder of why they're important and meaningful?

9. How often is producing the highest quality output your dominant motive rather than task completion?

PART II: DESCRIBE

For the following questions, describe how you would most likely respond. To get the most from your efforts, don't describe what you think you should do, but rather what you would most likely do based on how you've responded to similar situations in the past.

Outline whether and how the following statement describes your current efforts, "Consider how many ways you or people around you design mechanisms to muscle through or increase an activity's quantity without tackling the heart of where the difference really occurs — quality through meaningfulness?"

DISCOVERY SECTION

Consider the statement "All meaningful activities are important, but not all-important activities are meaningful. You don't have to love the activity — just the reason why you do it. Then rote motions give way to dynamic purpose." and outline whether and how this describes your current approach.

PRACTICE ACTIVITIES SECTION

Compare two scenarios from your recent experiences — one more and one less successful. How did you anchor or overlook meaningfulness in the action? How did you emphasize quantity or quality?

- Experience #1 — More Successful

- Experience #2 — Less Successful

DISCOVERY SECTION

Generally, what patterns can you identify when you're likely to anchor the meaningfulness of your actions? When you focus most on quality?

CHAPTER 4

THE **SHAPER** CYCLE

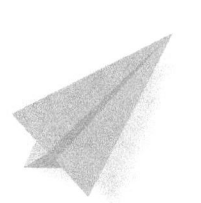

Actions can differ wildly from what is anticipated. That's what a group of novice adventurers discovered in the Colorado backcountry. Planning to spend the day exploring, they drove to a remote wilderness outcropping around noon, strapped on their daypacks, and set off hiking. As the sun fell, they found themselves in a struggle for survival.

Grasping that they were in trouble came slowly at first, and then all at once. Starring into the dense vegetation of the Rocky Mountain wilderness, the group realized what no one wants to: they were lost. As the group worked their way along an overgrown path, they deviated and accidentally trekked deep into the forest's underbelly. It was a dark, overcast night making visibility nearly impossible.

Light on provisions and knowledge of the local terrain and about 10 kilometers from their vehicles — while nearly three times that far from the nearest town — a casual excursion had become something much more serious. Even in late summer, the nighttime temperatures in the Colorado highlands routinely fall below freezing. The group had no winter or sleeping gear and just two flashlights among them. With each passing hour their prospects worsened.

By midnight, panic began to take hold of some in the group. Fatigued and uncomfortable, smart people put forward jumbled thoughts and emotions that exacerbated the situation. They credit others in the group for delivering them all from the terrible situation.

Talking with several of those who survived the event, it's clear that while they all experienced the same circumstances, their mindsets at the time were very different. Thoughts for some turned to frustrated, then hopeless places that crippled their ability to produce solutions. Others were able to repurpose their thinking to eventually realize that the group had mistakenly veered at what they thought was a camouflaged trail fork and carved a near semi-circle path around their vehicles. A straight line cut through its radius would lead them to safety.

Neither pattern of thought was random. And both achieved just what it intended.

One of the survivors described the mentality of those who saved the group that night.

> "It was more than just staying calm. I know they were worried, too, but I'm glad they handled it differently. At the time it seemed annoying and, a little absurd, but one man specifically kept telling us we're going to figure this out and describing what he was going to do the next day with his family. He just wouldn't come off that line of thinking regardless of what others said."

There is no discernible genetic pattern to who responded in which way. Some very successful and intelligent people went to dark places. Others, who no one in the group previously considered naturally gifted, processed the situation distinctly — more like a puzzle to be solved than a determined fate. While both groups were scared, tired, and hungry, the latter was able to trigger a chain of positive effects. Without knowing what to call it, they employed a Shaper process that can be predicted and repeated.

The word Shaper is significant when used with mindset because it describes that the two are inextricably linked. Mindset is a group of thoughts that are situationally variable — not inherent or permanent. It can be molded (particularly outside of semi-autonomous functions). And learning to effectively position one's mindset largely determines outcomes.

Arranging your thoughts in a particular way at any given time ignites a series of physiological responses that impact engagement attitudes — where activity quality is largely influenced. That's why talented people who could have thrived in that tough situation in the Colorado wilderness broke down when their thoughts betrayed them, and others shaped their thinking to kindle a positive response.

This isn't unlike the findings of researchers at Cal-Berkeley who asked, *do we smile instinctively because we're happy or does the act of smiling contribute to our happiness?* They found significant support for the latter.

When you paste on a smile there is something at work that is pretty amazing: facial expressions themselves can actually make us feel. If you wrinkle your nose and narrow your eyes as you would if you were really angry, your body will release some adrenaline and your heart rate may speed up as if you were actually angry. The same thing is true for other emotions. This means that sometimes we should just smile, even if we don't feel like it. As horribly forced as that sounds, there is solid science to back up the notion that this will, in fact, make us feel happier.[40]

Replace smiling with certain patterns of thought and happiness with other purposeful emotions and a similar effect emerges. By considering the impact these patterns have on setting into motion a ripple effect of engagement attitude, activity quality, and, ultimately, desired outcomes, the ingredients to a remarkable cycle takes shape.

THE SHAPER CYCLE

There are four phases in the Shaper cycle: mindset, engagement, action, and outcome. It's helpful to think of the first two primarily as triggers and the others as their dependent results. Described in detail over the next several pages, their priority and direction matter tremendously.

Mindset is the epicenter of productivity — your mindset impacts your level of engagement. Engagement level is what largely determines input quality, so effectively understanding and influencing this cycle is crucial. Action quality is a leading predictor of outcomes, more so than quantity, so focusing exclusively on behaviors and activities tends to under produce. Ordering matters. When certain phases are overemphasized or others bypassed, desired results tend to act like sand in your hand — they're elusive.

Said another way, our beliefs largely derive from our thoughts. And, action biology – both constructive and destructive — largely follows our

---

[40] Carter, C. (2009, 2014). http://greatergood.berkeley.edu/raising_happiness/ post/fake_it_till_you_make_it. Retrieved September 2, 2015.

beliefs. Our thoughts are the catalyst to a powerful and, in ways reserved to the wonder of human physiology, near instantaneous sequence of biological responses. In the split moment between external stimulus and response lies agency and choice – our ability to shape subsequent beliefs and actions through our mindset. These choices are positively or negatively fortified through our thoughts. Propensity toward anger can shift to patience through intentional Shaping. And deep-seeded biases can give way to empathy and understanding by successfully harnessing the Shaper cycle. Perhaps most importantly, prevailing engagement attitudes can elevate from negative-leaning or resistant to positive reinforcing quickly and sustainably.

Figure 3 on the next page helps you to visualize the mindset Shaper cycle and how the various elements in the cycle interact.

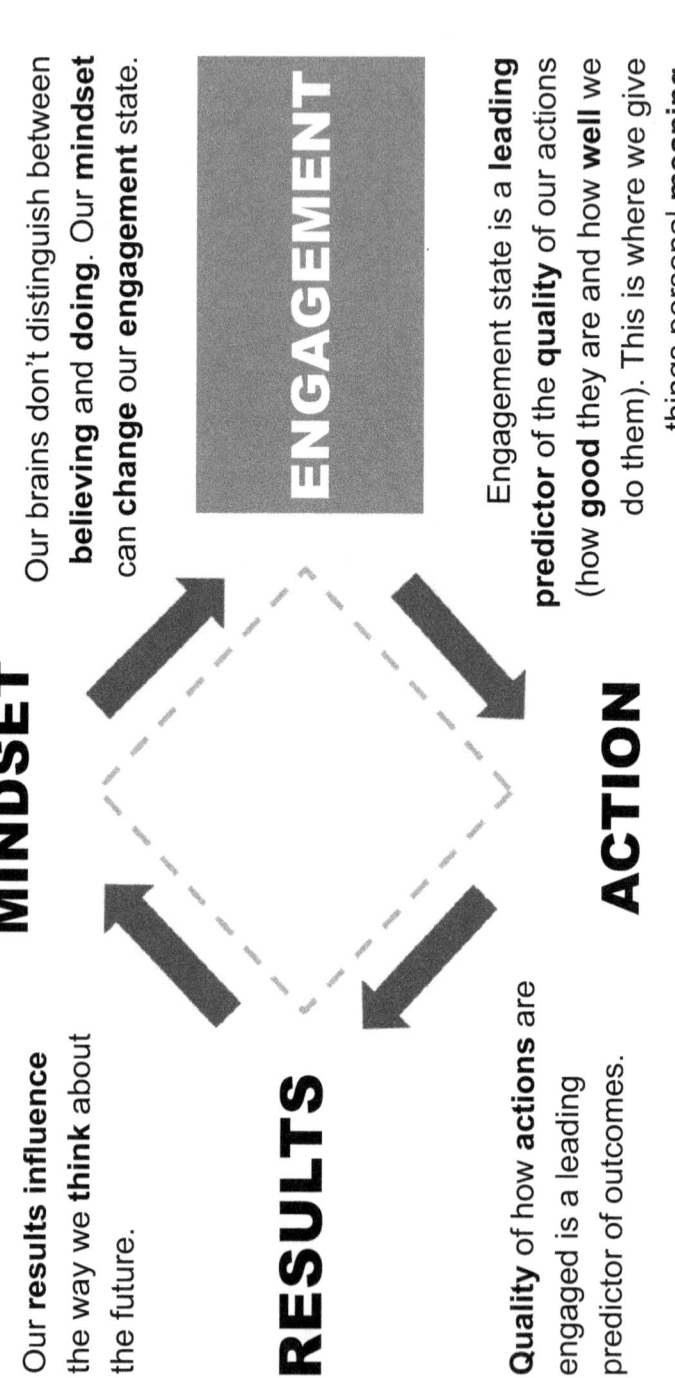

Figure 3 - Shaper Cycle

MINDSET

When YouTube violinist sensation Lindsey Sterling was asked, "You're very comfortable owning the spotlight. Any tips that [others] should know?" she gave an incredibly salient response supported by years of neurological research.

"Visualization—it's been huge for me. Your mind doesn't know the difference between imagination and reality. You can't always practice perfectly—my fingers will play a little bit out of tune or my dance moves might not be as sharp—but in my mind I can practice perfectly. Then it will be familiar to your brain."[41]

More than nice thoughts, the focused eye sees how thinking and doing intimately relate. The brain is beautifully intricate, but surprisingly simple. It is wired to process thinking about and actually experiencing an event in similar ways.[42][43][44][45] This is why recalling an uncomfortable experience or personalizing a fictional film can ignite intense responses — as if you're living the event — despite knowing the experience isn't actually happening. Because thinking and doing travel a similar mental pathway, patterns of thought have tremendous influence on actions. In the split second between impression and brain response, our thoughts impact how our brain functions.

Approximately 95% of our actions are motivated by our subconscious mind - reinforcing how vital it is to align your mindset with who and where you want to be. Intentionally inserting certain thoughts, symbols,

---

41 http://www.glamour.com/inspired/2015/12/lindsey-stirling-highest-earning- female-youtuber. Retrieved December 9, 2015.

42 Jenkins, A. C., Dodell-Feder, D., Saxe, R., & Knobe, J. (2014). The Neural Bases of Directed and Spontaneous Mental State Attributions to Group Agents. PloS one, 9(8), e105341.

43 Saxe, R., & Young, L. (2013). Theory of Mind: How brains think about thoughts. The handbook of cognitive neuroscience, 204-213.

44 Bernhardt, B. C., & Singer, T. (2012). The neural basis of empathy. Neuroscience, 35(1), 1.

45 Saarela, M. V., Hlushchuk, Y., Williams, A. C. D. C., Schürmann, M., Kalso, E., & Hari, R. (2007). The compassionate brain: humans detect intensity of pain from another's face. Cerebral cortex, 17(1), 230-237.

and visuals into your mindset prompts the brain to redirect resources to positive reinforcing functions.[46]

An exercise conducted with managers on four continents from companies like HP, Pfizer, Telekom, Movistar, SAP and GM to demonstrate how thought Shaper can influence new idea generation. Participants are shown the picture of a woman in a normal retail shopping setting and asked to describe an innovation to improve her experience. No further instructions are given. Regardless of demographic or country, responses are predictable. Some struggle to come up with anything and conclude that they're not creative. Their thoughts tend to be negative reinforcers — worried about what they can't do or don't see. Most of the other participants design innovations that are incremental, common, and oblivious to the cues from the woman in the picture. They struggle to adapt, automatically reaching for familiar ideas they've formed over years of experience that color how they process even new events.

Without providing innovation hints or ideas, we then do a series of mental framing techniques with the group. One is technical — it expands one's conceptual framework by building a bigger box around the scenario (considering its before, during, and after implications). The other helps participants to think about what they think about. By recognizing one's current mindset, it's easier to embrace congruent statements that elevate to an invested mindset.

Participants are again shown the picture. Like turning on a light, creativity fills the room as they imagine the picture in new ways and empathize with what it represents. That thinking allows them to do things they couldn't do previously. By burning new neuropaths through conscious thought and vivid imagining, they see potential for a new reality — and their actions follow.

Now picture a pathway that is worn, potholed, and somewhat unkempt. This is a mindset that defaults to routine, negative, or mimic responses.

---

46 Mindset is defined here as groups of thoughts that influence situational response and interpretation. There are many forces that influence one's mindset, including environment. In our observations, however, that relationship is not entirely deterministic.

Full of potential, it's not well tended. Environment and passive circumstance steal more than their share of the mental real estate. Rote reactions displace thoughtfulness — especially when the stakes are high or new. And performance is compromised.

All else equal, shaping your thinking to carve out desired paths does at least two things. First, it better predicts that you'll take that path because you've actively invested in creating it. Just as magnets attract metal, certain patterns of thought entice doing. An invested mindset didn't casually select some of those hikers in Colorado. They anchored their thoughts to positive reinforcers, which broadened their capacity to uncover solutions.

Second, because thinking and doing travel a related mental road, when combined with emotional engagement, what you do tends to yield similar results to what you envision.

ENGAGEMENT

If mindset is the vehicle in the Shaper process, purposeful engagement[47] is the fuel. Together they catalyze action quality. Think of this as combining the cognitive and emotional elements of the human experience. You think of how to interpret a situation, and the brain employs emotions to get the rest of your body to act accordingly.

In daily language, emotion is experiencing strong feeling. Tapping emotion provides the *why* to activities. It's what makes things meaningful.

For example, there is no functional justification for the price of a consumer diamond. Sure, it is unique among minerals, but a diamond doesn't nourish or replenish. It won't keep you warm and it can't provide shelter. Yet, it's priced above most substances. This is almost entirely because of the emotion attached to diamonds. They are symbolic of love.

---

47 To simplify, engagement and attitude are often used interchangeably.

The word symbolic matters. *Humans don't love actual objects or events or people, we love the way we feel when we're around them.* The symbol is a reminder of that sensation. That's why emotion is so important to understand and effectively tap — it gives purpose to and largely determines how well something is done.

Brain imaging describes why this is the case. You're more likely to vividly perceive, recall, and respond to things that are emotionally anchored. Researchers express this as a 'flash bulb that illuminates an event as it's captured for memory.'[48] Whereas, mundane facts, activities, events, or objects don't spur the same effect.

Engagement is emotional commitment — a particular state of being. Remember the first time you learned or taught someone to drive a manual stick shift vehicle? Chances are there was a lot of lurching and breaking and stalling, at first. Frustration became stress, and even fear. Then you found your rhythm as mind and body response began to put the gears where they needed to be. Engagement is when thinking and feeling become productive doing. There are two common deceptions regarding emotional engagement. The first is that emotion can be bypassed and exceptional results still achieved. Because emotion is often viewed as irrational or uncontrollable (simplistically associated with outward manifestations like crying or anger rather than inner drive), the temptation is to discount its role in performance. It seems easier and more calculated to cut it out and exclusively focus on which activities to do and how often to do them — as if humans are a mechanical process.

There's a dilemma to that reasoning. Quantity alone is a poor predictor of success; doing more of something without accounting for the level of emotional involvement can actually reduce quality — which is a strong predictor of success. Doing a lot of something is a poor substitute for doing something well. Despite rationality's growing celebrity — it's incomplete.

---

48 Todd, R. M., Talmi, D., Schmitz, T. W., Susskind, J., & Anderson, A. K. (2012). Psychophysical and neural evidence for emotion-enhanced perceptual vividness. The Journal of Neuroscience, 32(33), 11201-11212.

Skipping emotional engagement in the Shaper process and going straight to activity regulation is like the child who covers his eyes and thinks no one can see him. He thinks he's clever, but his approach is deeply flawed.

The advice to 'remove emotion from it' is not only impossible, it's counterproductive. The better guidance is to understand and turn emotion to your advantage.

The other deception is that emotion is only passive. An event happens and emotion naturally flows from it. A useful term for this is *when, then* logic. "When I get a promotion then I'll feel satisfied." Research suggests the opposite. You're more likely to get the promotion because you were emotionally engaged, which led to better work. Front loading effective emotional engagement helps to drive desired outcomes.

Think back to the Jason Lezak Olympic experience. In an interview following the event, he beautifully described the interplay between mindset and emotional engagement. He also showed that the effect can be sweeping and nearly instantaneous.

As his teammate touched the wall, Lezak knifed into the pool to complete the relay's final leg. Lezak's own words are extremely telling as he describes what then took place.

> *Reporter:* So, let's talk about the Olympic finish for a second, everyone is talking about this.
>
> *Lezak:* I didn't think it was possible. When I dove in I was behind, this guy was a world record holder. He had a whole-body length on me.
>
> *Reporter:* When you dove into the water, you were in the last leg of the competition. When you dove into the water you saw you guys were losing. What was going through your mind?
>
> *Lezak:* It's funny because normally when I swim I don't think about that many things. This time when I dove in, first instinct was "Oh my gosh I think I might have false started. I was, so anxious I just

wanted to get into that water, I was behind. So that went through my head a little bit. Then I got to the half-way down and I saw how far ahead he was and I had some negative thoughts there, too. I was like wow this is impossible, this guy's too far ahead.... world record holder. But I had to turn that into some positive thoughts obviously.

Reporter: Thoughts.

Lezak: Exactly! So, by the time I got about halfway back 25 left you know I had this surge of adrenaline. I was really pumped and I felt like this was really possible.[49]

The untrained eye is tempted to chalk up achievement to chance or superior talent, but that's too simplistic. The opposing French swimmer was equally or more talented and also finished in world-class time. Even Lezak swam two different races — one moderate lap and one incredible lap.

The smarter bet is to look at how Lezak at once positioned his mindset to unleash positive emotions that helped him to surge forward. Before that, he hadn't made up much ground. No matter how badly Lezak wanted to win, had he failed to strategically engage mentally or simply told himself to swim harder, the result almost certainly would have been different.

What was actually happening — why did it work? Is this effect reserved for momentous events or gifted Olympians? Because of how the human mind is wired, Shaper can work with just about anything.

Take family pictures. Many people love to hate them (especially husbands). They require a lot of planning, they're long, and the end product isn't always what you'd hoped.

Envision you're a parent and one sunny Saturday morning a car strikes your young daughter — killing her. You rush to her aid, but it's too late. There's nothing you can do but cling to her lifeless body — and beg the heavens to give her back. That family picture is the last image you have

---

49   https://www.youtube.com/watch?v=A1ussHesFgs. Retrieved August 1, 2015.

of your sweet family together. How glad are to have that photo with your beautiful girl? Given perspective, how easy is it to let the pettiness you associated with family pictures melt away?

Imagine beginning your next family picture session with a sense of gratitude for the time you have with your family to capture that memory. Same experience (family pictures), completely different outlook. Your mindset can change your emotional attitude, which can prompt entirely more productive behavior.

Just as in physics weight (w=mg) is always present, emotion can't be cut out of the human experience. So, it's crucial to point it in the right direction. Emotional indifferentness tends to be a reactive state that derails outcomes. "I dislike family pictures; therefore, this won't be a good experience." "I'll power through this so I can get to the next thing." You half-heatedly check off a task, passively accept whatever comes from an event, or pre-determine that something will disappoint. Your mindset is either on auto-pilot or counterproductive.

Whereas, using your mindset to front-load positive emotion into your efforts tends to catalyze returns.

ACTION

Passive and active experiences are very different. Facebook behavior is a good example. Remember, busy doesn't equal productive, and formulaic routines are poor proxy for genuine engagement. Psychologist Maria Konnikova explains why this is the case.

> In every study that distinguished the two types of Facebook experiences—active versus passive—people spent, on average, far more time passively scrolling through newsfeeds than they did actively engaging with content. Demands on our attention lead us to use Facebook more passively than actively, and passive experiences, no matter the medium, translate to feelings of disconnection and boredom. We get bored, look at Facebook, and become more bored.

When our attention is actively engaged, we aren't bored. Getting rid of Facebook (however) wouldn't change the fact that our attention is, more and more frequently, forgetting the path to proper, fulfilling engagement. (Facebook's) the symptom.[50]

Too obsessed with posting about an experience to fully appreciate it. Listlessly scrolling through feeds while in social settings. Forming assumptions without thinking them through. Killing time rather than purposefully filling it. Preoccupation with external audiences. These, and many more, are ways passive experiencing demands time, steals resources, and appears busy — but doesn't really produce. Sidestepping authentic engagement nearly always misses the mark.

A similar effect takes place outside the simulated world of Facebook. Bypassing mindset and emotional engagement and going straight to activity regulation is like famed academic C.S. Lewis' description,

> "In a sort of ghastly simplicity, we remove the organ and demand the function. We make men without chests and expect of them enterprise. We castrate and bid the geldings be fruitful."[51]

Activities are just a mechanism between desired results (outputs) and meaningful engagement (inputs). They're the tool — not the finished product or the craftsman. Why would we expect desired results from extensive activity lists, goals, and statements that don't effectively involve the crucial inputs of mindset and emotional attitude?

This is why going through the motions is so common (and alarming). Auto-pilot, or passive experiencing, tends to kick in when activity or behavior regulation is the dominant theme. Activity or behavior regulation is a favorite managerial device when seeking better performance — but it actually creates tension between desired results and the strategy to achieve it. Fixating on strategic planning, daily activity monitoring,

---

50 http://www.newyorker.com/tech/elements/how-facebook-makes-us-unhappy. Retrieved September 5, 2015.
51 Lewis, C. S. (1947). The Abolition of Man.

metrics, and to-do lists absent of Shaper is like marching through the jungle without a guide. It's not a shortcut, it's a recipe for getting lost.

Falling prey to this trap helps to explain why similarly talented people can do the same activity — and get completely different results. Quality (whether measured as speed, accuracy, or intricacy) isn't rooted in getting an activity done, but in believing why it should be done well. Creativity, innovation, and other measures of superior performance depend on this ordering.

Getting the most out of one's activities begins with properly accounting for their arrangement in the Shaper cycle.

Shaper isn't about self-lying; it's a form of positive intelligence.[52] It won't make a professional basketball player of a 5'6 inch lab tech. But that's not its intent. Rather, done well it creates the conditions for that 5'6 inch intellectual to openly search his strengths and to honestly appraise ways and opportunities to employ them. And it prompts bold movement forward.

Not leaving outcomes to chance requires front loading effective emotional engagement through specific Shaper techniques. This first requires knowing to recognize the various levels of engagement. Then influencing efforts can be better predicted, implemented, and repeated.

---

52 Chamine, S. (2012). Positive intelligence: Why only 20% of teams and individuals achieve their true potential and how you can achieve yours. Greenleaf Book Group.

DISCOVERY SECTION

PART I: RESPOND

Respond to the questions below using the following rating scale:

A = Always. B = Often. C = Sometimes. D = Rarely. E = Never.

10. When seeking better results, how often do you begin with Shaper?

11. How often do you ascribe superior outcomes primarily to better talent or circumstance?

12. How often does your engagement attitude reflect mastery of the Shaper cycle?

PART II: DESCRIBE

For the following question, describe how you would most likely respond. To get the most from your efforts, don't describe what you think you should do, but rather what you would most likely do based on how you've responded to similar situations in the past.

You overhear a colleague state, "that person has a really bad attitude and isn't going to change." What are your thoughts about this statement?

_____
_____
_____
_____
_____
_____
_____
_____

DISCOVERY SECTION

Consider the statement "Activities are just a mechanism between desired results (outputs) and meaningful engagement (inputs). They're the tool — not the finished product or the craftsman. Why would we expect desired results from extensive activity lists, goals, and statements that don't effectively involve the crucial inputs of mindset and emotional attitude" and outline whether and how this describes your current approach.

PRACTICE ACTIVITIES SECTION

Compare two scenarios from your recent experiences — one more and one less successful. How did you view your own agency in the scenario? Even if you didn't know the process by name, how did Shaper influence the outcome?

- Experience #1 — More Successful

- Experience #2 — Less Successful

DISCOVERY SECTION

Generally, what patterns can you identify when you harness your engagement state to improve your activity quality?

DISCOVERY SECTION

Generally, what patterns can you identify when you harness your engagement state to improve your activity quality?

CHAPTER 5

THREE LEVELS OF ENGAGEMENT

Sometimes history is written correctly the first time. Other times it needs re-examining. After British scholar Jonathan Fennell meticulously analyzed letters to friends and family by Britain's 8th army stationed in Northern Africa prior to General Bernard Montgomery's arrival — history received a much needed revision.

The story prior to Fennell's work read like a tired piece of propaganda. The troops were generally in good spirits. Though a series of personnel changes had been made, it was reported that general esteem for leadership among the troops was on solid footing. Well-trained and resourced, the British 8th army was just one victory away from a turning point on the African front.

Only the part about needing a victory was accurate. Morale among the troops prior to Montgomery's arrival was abysmal. Their letters, sickness rates, and psychological profiles reveal a group on the brink of disaster. In a sort of desperate, private honesty they wrote to friends and family of their disaffectedness; they didn't want to fight and many preferred to surrender. Equally noteworthy, many wrote more confidentially and affectionately about the opposing German general, Erwin Rommel, than they did of their own leaders.[53]

Prior to Montgomery's arrival, the British approach in Africa lacked clarity. Leaders gave similar energy to devising plans for retreat as they did plans for attack. Commitment was fractured, disjointed. And the soldiers knew it — despite what was portrayed publicly. Montgomery found a group of men he would quickly understand didn't know their directive, didn't appreciate their role in the effort, and who sensed that retreat was a likely alternative.

That would change quickly.

For his challenges in other areas and even in the direst circumstances, Montgomery had a keen ability to perceive the engagement level of his troops — and then elevate it through affecting their mindset. His

---

53 Fennell, J. (2011). Combat and morale in the North African campaign: the Eighth Army and the path to El Alamein. Cambridge University Press.

first address to Senior Officers upon arriving in Africa underscores this approach.

"You do not know me. I do not know you. [But] we must understand each other and have confidence in each other. I have confidence in you. We will work together as a team. And together we will gain the confidence of this great Army and go forward to final victory in Africa. I don't like the general atmosphere I find here. It is an atmosphere of doubt, of looking back to select the next place for withdrawal. We will stand here and fight. I have no intention of launching our great attack until we are ready and you can rest assured on that point. The great point to remember is that we are going to finish with this chap Rommel once and for all. There is no doubt about it."[54]

Montgomery would go on to explain,

> "I made the soldiers partners with me in the battle. I always told them what I was going to do and what I wanted them to do. I think the soldiers felt that they mattered and that they belonged."[55]

Though very much aware of the lack of physical preparation among the 8th army and the pressing need for further training and planning, Montgomery showed remarkable restraint — and savvy — by not first launching into a series of activity commands. Instead he began with assessing — and then elevating — the mindset of the group. That was his multiplier. By accurately diagnosing their level of engagement, he could tailor his approach to have a more profound effect.

It worked. Despite no appreciable changes in armaments, the 8th army proved decisive victors on the African front — an important inflection point to the war.

Montgomery seemed to have seen that outcome from the start.

---

54 http://www.wjinst.com/wjinst/bios/leadmont.htm. Retrieved 22 December 2015.
55 Adair, J. (2010). Strategic leadership: How to think and plan strategically and provide direction. Kogan Page Publishers.

"After having an easy war, things have now gotten much more difficult," Montgomery once said to a colleague prior to the series of victorious offensives. His colleague told him to take heart, to cheer up. "I'm not talking about me; I'm talking about Rommel."[56]

THE SOUTHWEST SECRET

What Montgomery understood is not secret, but it is surprisingly rare. As the pendulum over-swings in the direction of rationality and activity regulation (not alone bad, but incomplete) an unintended dichotomy takes shape. Numbers and statistics replace awareness of human experiencing — rather than supporting and enriching it. In our observation those people and groups who are able to put each in its proper order realize a performance advantage.

Take Southwest Airlines. It's not by accident that they set the industry standard for innovation and financial performance. While data drives much of their efforts, this doesn't fully distinguish them because that's also the case for their competitors.

It is a more humanized analytic, recruiting for and training their people to effectively identify and tap the levels of emotional engagement, that is a key differentiator for the firm.

A colleague's email describing his experience on a Southwest flight gives a snapshot of this principle. It also shows how one person who embodies this skill can redeem otherwise tenuous situations.

He was traveling with an associate to Alabama on business. Not a frequent Southwest flyer, he reluctantly agreed to take the airline because the person he traveled with insisted. There were things he thought he liked and disliked about the firm. He knew of Southwest's reputation for personalized customer service and their innovative approach to flying, but he didn't like the thought of having to race for his seat. His

---

56 Fennell, J. (2011). Combat and morale in the North African campaign: the Eighth Army and the path to El Alamein. Cambridge University Press.

experience was with assigned seating, so he was sure he would end up next to the bathroom or wedged between two large men for four hours.

His friend assured him that his boarding number would make them among the first to claim their seats. Getting to board with his friend was a big deal to this colleague. As the ticket agent belted over the loud speaker that it was time to board his anxiety grew.

Hearing the announcement, our colleague's friend stood up and signaled for him to follow.

As the line started to move, this man's anxiety grew. His mind raced with thoughts of wishing he had an assigned seat and rehearsing what he would say if he was found boarding out of turn.

In his words,

> "Something about my appearance must have betrayed me — my zealousness to appear calm must have come off as the opposite — because as I approached the counter to board, I was told to step aside and wait. I immediately began to sweat and I sang like a canary. I have never flown Southwest before, and my friend said I could board with him. Unsuccessful I quietly slipped to the end of the line and waited to be the last person to board.

As I re-approached the gate as the last to board, I waited for the person in front of me to gain some distance between us so that I could privately save face for what I considered an innocent faux pas.

That's not what the counter agent had in mind. As he watched the person in front of me stride beyond the point of hearing his comments, he turned to me and said sharply: 'So you think you are better than everybody?' His words took a moment for me to compute. All I could initially muster was 'What?' and then a quick 'no, I don't think I am better than everybody' to which he replied 'Just get on the plane, sir.'

I felt numb — his words were so unexpected. I tried to champion my case by explaining again that I had never flown Southwest before and that my friend." I was cutoff with an abrupt 'Get on the plane.' Now my embarrassment boiled into something else, 'You can't speak to me like that, do you think you are better than me?' I said. His reply pounded into my chest like a sucker punch 'I know I am better than you!' 'You can't talk to another person that way' I lectured "You are no better than me and I am not better than you" was my declaration.

> "Oh, I know I am better than you". I demanded to speak to his manager immediately. 'No,' and he walked away. Fearing missing my flight, I walked down the jet way, but vowed that I would never fly Southwest again and that I would lob a formal complaint at the firm at the first opportunity.

As I approached the plane and the line of the last few stragglers waiting to face their fate of middle seats and armrest jockeying, I saw the flight attendant welcoming guests.

She clearly sensed my frustration, confirmed by my mumblings about the horrible experienced I'd just had. She motioned for me to step aside to have a semi private conversation in the corner of the cabin. She began first by asking; 'tell me what happened.'

I explained that I had been treated disrespectfully for what was a simple misunderstanding. I felt unimportant and devalued. She put her hand on my shoulder and said I shouldn't have been treated that way. But then she did something more. With all the caring of her 50 something years, she said,

> 'It is the beginning of the day and you've had something awful happen to you, but don't you dare let him take this day from you.' She went on: 'If you let him take this day from you then he wins and you deserve to have a great day.'

She told me that I seemed like a good man and that I was not the type of person that was going to let someone rob me of being that man. Her words sunk in deeply.

Stubbornly, I made one final attempt to hold on to my right to be offended and retorted: 'but he shouldn't have treated me that way.' She patiently looked at me and said "I know, but we are better than that."

I felt my anger and offense melt like ice exposed to the sun. She kindly guided me to my seat and assured me that if I needed anything at all, she would be right there for me.

After a glare at my friend for abandoning me at the gate and failing to save me a seat, I spent the rest of the flight thinking about what this woman had said.

Her words sent me on my own meaningful mental paths; how could I better help others move from an indifferent state to a feeling of value and importance?

By the end of the flight, my mindset was completely altered. In just a few moments of conversation, this beautiful person rescued me from an indifferent state, and then elevated me to something much more useful. I thought of others who are wronged (or whom I'd wronged), real or perceived, and how I might be a catalyst for change for them.

I couldn't deny that I hated how I felt during the initial confrontation and loved how I felt when I was around this woman and as I sat in my seat thinking of the opportunities around me to influence the engagement of others. Though I was sure she had done something similar with hundreds of other people, her approach made me feel like she had handcrafted it just for me.

As I departed the plane, she again pulled me aside and side-hugged me. With her hand on my arm, she genuinely asked 'Feel better?'

'Yes.'

Sensing I was in a much different place than she found me, she left me with a challenge,

'Now go out and make today great.'

"I promised myself that I would."

LEVELS OF ENGAGEMENT

Engagement is a function of emotion–a catalyzing force that is directly affected by mindset. It largely determines an activity's productive quality. Because engagement is more easily observed than thoughts, pinpointing its state is key to Shaper efforts. Accurately diagnose engagement and the opportunity to affect it follows.

Concepts related to human behavior are aided by boundaries. There are three primary levels of engagement. As the world grows more complex and behaviorally intensive, knowing how to identify and effectively influence these states of engagement is the new competitive advantage.

Before describing each level, it's important to note that engagement occurs on a fluid spectrum and can be influenced up and down — often quickly. Rather than a fixed trait, engagement relies on situational perception and interpretation; it is impacted by effectively altering how events are perceived and interpreted. This was evident in the Southwest example as the flight attendant was able to employ specific strategies to help a customer quickly move from a negative state to a more positive one.

Second, engagement infuses all aspects of life–you can't choose to not participate. What you can choose is how well you will participate. Because engagement is perception sensitive, it can be fickle, and different approaches for each of the three levels are required to have the desired effect. Congruence is key (treated in detail in a subsequent chapter). Taking Shaper actions best suited for one level and applying them to another can have frustrating, even disastrous, outcomes.

While each of these levels (and how to affect them) are discussed in greater detail in the next chapters, they're introduced as a group here to outline their sequencing.

LEVELS OF ENGAGEMENT

		PERFORMANCE OUTCOME
INDIFFERENT	CHARACTERIZED BY GENERAL DISBELIEF THAT YOUR ACTIONS ARE IMPORTANT OR MEANINGFUL OR THAT OTHERS VIEW THEM THE SAME. AN INDIFFERENT STATE IS ACCOMPANIED BY THOUGHTS OF AMBIVALENCE, MARGINALIZATION, MISTRUST, OR DOUBT. PRIMARY DRIVERS ARE GUILT AND FEAR.	Below Expectations
INTERESTED	CHARACTERIZED BY GENERAL BELIEF THAT SOMETHING BETTER IS POSSIBLE. VIEWS ACTIVITIES AS OPPORTUNITIES & TOOLS RATHER THAN REQUIREMENTS. HAPPY WITH RESULTS, BUT NOT SATISFIED. SEES POTENTIAL IN TAKING WELL-CONSIDERED RISKS. LEVERAGES STRENGTHS. EFFICIENT. RESULTS EQUAL ENERGY EXERTED.	Meets Expectations
INVESTED	CHARACTERIZED BY CONNECTEDNESS TO A PURPOSE, LEARNING, AND THE DESIRE TO STRETCH THE BOUNDARIES OF POSSIBLE IN VALUABLE WAYS. ATTRACTS INPUT WELL AND OFTEN. RESILIENT TO UNFOUNDED REJECTION. SEES WELL-CONSIDERED RISK AS POSITIVE AND NECESSARY. SEEKS VALUABLE ADVANTAGES. ACTIVITY QUALITY IS ADVANCED AND ORIGINAL. ACHIEVES MORE WITH LESS.	Outstanding

Figure 4

INDIFFERENT

The first level is indifferent. In this state people experience a general disbelief or lack understanding that what they are doing is important and meaningful. Environment and circumstances (external forces) are overly weighted. A common view is that people are beholden to these forces rather than agents within them. Those in both the General Montgomery and Southwest Airlines examples began at this level. There was an expectation gap to overcome. To those in an indifferent state their initial responses may seem real despite tuned-in outsiders recognizing them as irrational, distorted (seeing things that aren't there and not seeing things that are) or counterproductive. And, cynicism tends to prevail.

Activities conducted in an indifferent state often drain resources and fail to meet expectations. Recognizing this was part of Montgomery's brilliance. He knew that his soldiers' mindset needed to be affected (which would influence their emotional engagement) before he could expect their activities to improve. By getting the ordering right, he dramatically impacted the 8th army's course.

Indifference is primarily rooted in exaggerated guilt or fear; overweighting a perceived offense or threat or the lack of belief in a potential outcome. Thought indicators include (often correlated with comparable body language),

"This isn't for me."
"I'll never make it."
"I can't keep this up."
"It doesn't matter."
"Someone else can do this."
"They don't get it."
"I can't believe they'd do that."
"This will never work."
"Try to stay off the radar."

Those in an indifferent state perform below expectations. Provided they are capable of the task at hand — their mindset, and its impact on their level of engagement, is most commonly the explanation.

INTERESTED

Moving beyond indifference is interested. This is where the majority of people plateau – most of the time. This level is characterized by your current state of affairs.[57] It would be incorrect to think of this state as lazy or absent. The opposite is true. Here the emphasis is on completing tasks, often in high quantity, but without giving significant consideration to activity quality. Learning is overshadowed by thoughts of reinforcing routines.

Days are viewed like grocery lists, full of items to be checked off. Routine rules supreme and thoughts tend to contain snippet-like pep-talks — emphasizing getting through things or preserving status,

"I just have to do it."
"I've got this figured out."
"I'll do this until I can do that."
"They can't fire me if I do the work."
"Think of the possibilities"
"I can get through this–this is just a small part of my life."
"Just do what's required."

Another key sign of the interested state is risk orientation. Because interested's primary driver is to maintain status quo, tremendous effort is exerted to reject anything that hints of risk — no matter how well-founded. Fear of rejection is a strong, sometimes paralyzing, undercurrent in the interested state.

While the interested state tends to meet expectations, an honest appraisal reveals that this comes at a cost. More energy and resources are required to achieve less.

---

[57] Beck, R. and Harter, J. (2015). Managers Account for 70% of Variance in Employee Engagement. Gallup Business Journal. Retrieved 8 July 2015.

INVESTED

An important transition takes place between interested and invested. The possibility of something better begins to be the dominant thought. This is where QN (quantity) as the driving force gives way to QL (quality). Rather than requirements to complete, activities are viewed as opportunities and tools. Improvement is a dominant theme in this invested state; greater capacity and development is scouted within oneself and others. Learning is viewed as an opportunity to refine rather than an attack on existing norms. Mindfulness takes root and uniqueness is embraced over passive mimicry.

Thoughts in the invested state are characterized as happy with results, but not satisfied. This orientation informs how one views well-founded risk. Rather than something to be avoided, potential is seen in seeking new ways of doing things or better ways of doing existing things.

The words attributed to the former U.S. Supreme Court Justice (Potter Stewart) when describing thresholds "I know it when I see it" provide the first level of diagnostic support for this mindset. Invested engagement looks and acts very different from the other levels. Ideas are richer, more frequent, and better grounded in real opportunities. Defensiveness gives way to the desire for refinement. Neither delusional nor pessimistic, thought patterns appreciate existing resources and circumstance and then reimagine them in a better form. Interactions are authentic and productive. And marking time is replaced by committed effort.

Moving a layer deeper reveals another telling characteristic. Quality is the dominant motive. Rather than simply going through a series of tasks or avoiding them altogether, those in an invested state actively think about what they think about. Their actions are informed by the conscious decision to position them as effectively as possible — to create valuable advantages. Being invested manifests as connection to *why* beyond selfish designs (a substantive *because*; something beyond superficial praise), curiosity, and the desire to learn and stretch the boundaries of what is possible. It attracts input well (openly and from credible sources) and often. It is resilient to unfounded rejection. Well-considered risk is viewed as positive and necessary for growth. Thoughts are consistent with agents on environments rather than victims of it.

The invested state tends to achieve more with less, multiplying efforts rather than dividing them. Outcomes tend to outweigh the energy and resources expended. Done well, the performance results tend to be outstanding.

Below are common patterns of thought for those in an *invested* state,

> "I'm very grateful."
> "How can this add more value to others?"
> "Does this create sustained advantage?"
> "I want to share what has helped me."
> "There are great ideas out there and I'm going to find them."
> "Getting this right really matters."
> "Let's do things better – not just different"

When you do something great or see someone else doing something great and ask them how they did it they might not be able to explain the specific process, but chances are their motivating thoughts and attitudes looked very similar to these — prompting uncommon quality in their actions.

People in an invested state don't just see something. They intentionally shape their mindset *to see something*. Then they persist until hitting the mark. And remarkable things are more likely to result.

To understand how to better diagnose and influence each engagement state, the next two chapters dig deeper into each one — beginning at the first two levels: indifferent and interested.

DISCOVERY SECTION

PART I: RESPOND

Respond to the questions below using the following rating scale:

A = Always. B = Often. C = Sometimes. D = Rarely. E = Never.

13. When performing below or above expectation, how likely are you to recognize the influence of engagement?

14. How often do you accurately diagnose your level of engagement?

15. How often do you accurately diagnose the level of engagement of those around you?

PART II: DESCRIBE

For the following prompts, describe how you would most likely respond. To get the most from your efforts, **don't** describe what you *think you should do*, but rather *what you would most likely do* based on how you've responded to similar situations in the past.

You notice that someone you care for consistently says things like, "It's not that big a deal, anyway" or "I just have to power through this" when confronting challenging situations.

DISCOVERY SECTION

Consider the statement "Engagement is a function of emotion–a catalyzing force that is directly affected by mindset. It largely determines an activity's productive quality. Because engagement is more easily observed than thoughts, pinpointing its state is key to Shaper efforts. Accurately diagnose engagement and the opportunity to affect it follows" and outline whether and how this describes your current approach.

PRACTICE ACTIVITIES SECTION

Compare two scenarios from your recent experiences — one more and one less successful. Self-diagnose your level of engagement at the time. What cues helped you arrive at this determination?

- Experience #1 — More Successful

- Experience #2 — Less Successful

DISCOVERY SECTION

Given a similar scenario going forward, how could you build from the more successful elements and improve on the less successful ones?

DISCOVERY SECTION

Describe a personal experience with each of the three levels of engagement. What were your primary thought patterns in each?

- Indifferent

- Interested

DISCOVERY SECTION

- Invested

CHAPTER 6

CROSS THE **EXPECTATION** GAP

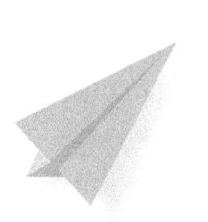

A group medical practice was undergoing tremendous change as it expanded and launched a new line of business. Stress was high. We were asked to do two things: assess the value of their strategy and to understand the impact of the changes on people within the firm.

We were given complete access to their financial reports and data analytics. We also received free rein to interview team members. Morale was low and interactions distant. The overwhelming sense among the group was that things were not going well.

The opposite was true. What we found was that the firm had never performed better. Yet the people within it had never felt worse. The owner-doctors were compensated more than ever before and the initial phase of the launch was going fine (encountering only challenges common to new initiatives), but a general sense of disconnectedness permeated the team.

A deeper dive explains why. Though the doctors were making significantly more (nearly 30% over their previous best year), they had secretly set their sights higher. This unwritten expectation led them to pressure staff more intensely — hawking over their activities, setting frequent meetings, communicating in short-demands, and ratcheting up urgency.

Ironically, even the doctors expressed frustration and dissatisfaction with their current state.

They were trapped in the mental gap of unrequited expectations. Chasing an ambiguous expectation was robbing them of the ability to appreciate their reality; they were actually doing tremendously better than what was already a highly successful practice, but couldn't appreciate that. And their responses contributed to indifference among the team — threatening the growth trend's sustainability.

FOOD RIOTS

Expectations are powerful forces that influence how people perceive events. Take riots in emerging markets. Talented researchers have painstakingly plotted global riots to look for commonalities.

Their first finding is uncommonly clean and straightforward for social science meta-analysis research.[58] Riots directly relate to food prices. When people are hungry, they're more likely to take to the street. Building on that work, what they found next is equally interesting.

Each food riot cluster, regardless of where it occurs in the world, is not an isolated event, but a direct response to the previous threshold. Controlling for other factors the impulse for people to riot updates based on their most recent experience. This occurs despite limited correlating changes in participant income, earning potential, or economic standing. Even when their reality doesn't appreciably change, their expectations do.

Let's look at a hypothetical example. The food index price in a given country is 150. No riot occurs. The food index the next year rises to 180 and social unrest grows — eventually spilling over into riots. 180 becomes the new expectation. Anything substantially different than that number is more likely to quickly trigger the next riot.

RAIN AND THE LOTTERY

If food riots are too distant from your daily living, the example of lottery activity and weather shows a similar effect — but in the opposite direction. Researchers at New York University found significant correlation between experiencing a positive event (when a less positive outcome was expected) and participation rates in the lottery.[59] The study

---

58 Lagi, M., Bertrand, K. Z., & Bar-Yam, Y. (2011). The food crises and political instability in North Africa and the Middle East. Available at SSRN 1910031.
59 Otto, A. R., Fleming, S. M., & Glimcher, P. W. (2016). Unexpected but incidental positive outcomes predict real-world gambling. Psychological science, 0956797615618366.

looked at two years' worth of daily lottery purchases in 174 New York City neighborhoods. Citywide gambling increased following unexpected sports wins and unusually sunny days. In other words, when people expect a less desirable outcome than what actually occurs, they're more likely to double down and try the lottery.

Though sporting event outcomes and weather have no rational bearing on likely lottery outcomes, experiencing a positive event that differs from what was expected — even if incidental — seems to imbue human behavior with belief.

REDIRECTING INDIFFERENCE

Understanding expectation dynamics is vital to accurately recognizing lower levels of engagement. Rarely is indifference a function of DNA. More often it is a distorted or disproportionate view of circumstances. Instead of starting indifferent, people get there, often quickly, in response to negatively perceived unmet expectations.

Marketing studies are a useful way to understand the onset of indifference. Think of consumer behavior. There's convincing research that engagement and disengagement are highly connected — prior levels of loyal engagement significantly influence customers' subsequent propensities to disengage.[60]

This means that people are more likely to grow indifferent when they've had a previous experience with something related to the current event or set of circumstances. Indifference isn't likely to happen in isolation — it's a response to current expectations based on previous experiences.

Accurately understanding when someone is indifferent and how that came to be is vital to changing the trend line. This presents an opportunity and an obstacle. The challenge relates to common practices. When a person

---

60 Bowden, J. L., Gabbott, M., & Naumann, K. (2015). Service relationships and the customer disengagement–engagement conundrum. Journal of Marketing Management, 31(7-8), 774-806.

is seen as indifferent a common instinct is to tell them to suck it up or to challenge (even threaten) them to get their act together.

Anyone who has been, raised, or interacted with teenagers can appreciate this tendency. The indifferent state tends to express as disinterest, ambivalence, or belligerence. Results are attributed to circumstance rather than agency (for example, contending that economic conditions don't allow for growth). Left unchecked, this mindset can see the bad in the good — fixating on the 1 negative experience rather than the 99 positive ones.

But what's at its roots? It's a void. A negative expectation gap — disbelief that the situation, and one's role in it, will turn out for the better. Related activities are viewed as unimportant and meaningless. Unfortunately, when someone is in an indifferent state what they're most likely to get from themselves and others is what they least likely need — an authoritarian challenge (such as 'work harder'). Because the gap is linked to a mental relationship with circumstance and emphasis on its negative parts — that approach to someone in an indifferent state is like asking them to throw punches against a brick wall.

Work ethic is rarely the underlying issue. It can take tremendous energy to be indifferent — even though that effort tends to be spent in unconstructive ways.

At its roots, the indifferent state doesn't believe that something's possible or the effort is worth it. That's also where the solution lies.

Indifference doesn't mean that people don't know the key activities to do. And, just because they're not doing them regularly doesn't mean they're incapable of doing them. What it does mean is that their belief that doing them well is important (essential) and meaningful (will make a difference) has diminished. Higher education is a common place to observe this phenomenon. How many students negatively or positively alter the quality of their work based on how they believe the professor perceives them?

Remember, thoughts influence engagement, which impacts action quality, which is predictive of results. So, well placed statements and interactions can have a significant elevating influence. By placing circumstance in its proper form — a description of events, not the inevitable prescription of responses — the opportunity for shaping appears.

What is needed is something that provides the opposite of the source of the gap: belief and reinforcement. Imagine the likely result for the soldiers of the 8th army had General Montgomery misdiagnosed their state and dogmatically challenged them — immediately sending them to battle before elevating their mindset. What is possible for the doctors from the chapter's opening example if they accurately diagnose the staff's state and move to re-instill belief in the importance and meaningfulness of their contribution?

Because the indifferent state is furthest removed from an invested mindset, the urge is to short-change the process by skipping steps. But that would be similar to running a marathon on two days training. It doesn't work.

The key is learning to spot how the indifferent state looks and then to position appropriately by taking the first step — to instill belief through recognition.

A brief example from home life shows how this can look. A teenage daughter makes a belligerent comment to her father and storms to her room, slamming the door in the process. The father's immediate instinct is to re-assert dominion — to compel the daughter to his will. He knows what she's capable of and wants to sharply challenge her in that direction.

Instead, he pauses. He thinks about what she's thinking about. She's clearly in an indifferent state. Rather than challenging her, he approaches her with love and expresses his belief in her. He recognizes what she is instead of emphasizing what she isn't (the latter being where her mindset is already focused). The anecdote is pure and specifically designed for the need, so even the most hardened of indifferent states will struggle to deflect this approach.

The result is someone elevated to the next state — now better suited to receive needed stimulation.

The data support this. Tracking our experiences with managers, when effectively imbued with belief and recognition following an indifferent episode nearly 90% demonstrated improved drive and determination — a vital measure of readiness for enhanced productivity.

For further evidence look at the vast majority of successful turnaround cases. From the return of Steve Jobs to Apple, to Lou Gerstner's efforts at IBM, to Priceline's resurgence after the tech crash of the early 2000's the re-establishment of belief in the company and people's stake in it is at the core. Those who try turnarounds without this fundamental understanding, shifting strategy without shoring up belief, find the headwinds to be extremely strong.[61][62][63][64][65][66]

Figure 5 provides a synopsis of the indifferent state, its underlying symptoms, and likely outcomes if left unattended. Similar to building muscle memory, effectively and frequently putting viable concepts sharpens your facility with them. Then, like a skilled physician, the initial observation of indifferent symptoms can be matched with the appropriate response.

---

61 Deutschman, A. (2001). The second coming of Steve Jobs. Currency.
62 Blumenthal, K. (2012). Steve Jobs: The man who thought different. Macmillan.
63 Slater, R. (1999). Saving big blue: Leadership lessons and turnaround tactics of IBM's Lou Gerstner. McGraw-Hill School Education Group.
64 Balgobin, R., & Pandit, N. (2001). Stages in the turnaround process:: The Case of IBM UK. European Management Journal, 19(3), 301-316.
65 Gerstner, L. V. (2002). Who says elephants can't dance?: inside IBM's historic turnaround. HarperCollins Publishers.
66 Nurse, K., Stephenson, S., & Mendez, A. (2017). Tourism, trade in services and global value chains. Future fragmentation processes: Effectively engaging with the ascendancy of global value chains, 135-156.

Mindset	Key activity perception	Behavioral indicators	Thought indicators	Results
Indifferent	Important **NO** Meaningful **NO**	Dreads engaging key activities Rarely seeks help Seeks to validate negativity Mainly driven by guilt or fear Sees risk taking as undesirable Feels misunderstood	"This isn't for me." "I'll never make it." "I can't keep this up." "It doesn't matter." "Someone else can do this." "They don't get it/me." "I don't want to"	Below Expectations

Figure 5

ELEVATING FROM INTERESTED

The engagement state above indifferent is *interested*. Think of this as content. It's the focus to maintain rather than advance. While not necessarily destructive, its opportunity cost is high.

Interested is the state where most people spend the majority of their time. The phenomenon is so pervasive that it has also been used to describe the strategic approach of industries, participants within them, and even countries.

For example, Harvard-featured research describes how countries can become interested about their resources.[67] Take Latin America. Among the most naturally endowed regions in the world, an interested approach

---

67 Moss Kanter, R. (2012). The business ecosystem: A country can become interested about its assets. The Harvard Magazine.

to these resources by some of its countries would be to primarily focus on the easy, readily understood, if less valuable process of commodity exploitation. Economic activity occurs, but at the cost of something more productive. This macro strategy then impacts what types of firms are attracted to or develop in the area, the countries' relationship with foreign direct investment, and the way the region's countries view designing efficient institutions and educating its population.

Let's look at another example — this one touching both the industry and individual levels. Despite producing the majority of the world's medical advancements, there are large pockets within the U.S. healthcare system that need repairing. Mental health treatment is one of them. Psychiatric researchers explain,

There are two gaps related to the provision of care: the gap between needing and entering formal care (the engagement gap) and, once a person is in care, the gap between receipt of low and high-quality care (the quality gap). Each year about 30% of Americans have a diagnosable mental disorder and are thought to need mental health care. Yet only about one-third of these persons become engaged in care, and only about one-third of these receive care of reasonably high quality. To illustrate the magnitude of these gaps: imagine that a population roughly equivalent to that of the four largest states combined (California, Texas, New York, and Florida) needs mental health care, but only those in California receive any care at all. And among Californians, only those living in Los Angeles County receive care of at least reasonable, not necessarily optimal, quality.[68]

This trend is not exclusive to mental health. Each year tens of thousands of people die from otherwise treatable cancer if detected early.[69] Fewer than 15% of those who have access to reasonable medical insurance engage in regular, preventative cancer screening.

---

68 Sullivan, G. (2015). Interested care and the quality gap. Psychiatric Services.
69 Siegel, R. L., Miller, K. D., & Jemal, A. (2015). Cancer statistics, 2015. CA: a cancer journal for clinicians, 65(1), 5-29.

Patients aren't the only ones in healthcare exhibiting complacent behavior. Cost for providers and participants rise yet generalized standard of care gains are negligible.

At the individual level there are several explanations for complacency, but two tend to present time and again.

Good is a strong impediment to great. In this state the tendency is to maintain the status quo. Think of the strong force routine can be in your daily life. The route you take to work, how you engage daily tasks, who you interact with, the types of conversations you have, where you eat, what you do when returning home from work, your level of observation throughout the day can all share the common root of change aversion.

Equilibrium and comfort are powerful influences. This is the sales person who learns to make more per transaction, but then stops seeking new clients because she's producing the same amount.

It is fallacy that passively habitual behavior requires little input or updating. It can take tremendous energy to maintain an interested state within a dynamic social world. And there is a high (though often underappreciated) cost to trying to remain in neutral.

Comfort seems desirable, but embraced excessively it shares more in common with stagnation than development.

Second, those in the interested state are aware of what needs to be done (important) but the sense of meaningfulness is fragile. Because of this, the driving force is obligation. Not wanting to let others down forms an awkward relationship with performance; the desire to meet expectations handcuffs one's ability to exceed them. In an odd way, imagining a different state seems like cheating on the current one.

While noble in part, rote obligation takes a toll. It relies on superficial expression rather than genuine interest. Perhaps more dangerous, when presented with significant change the interested state struggles to absorb or adapt to it. And it almost never originally contributes to it.

In short, this state takes hold because the risk or effort to do something else seems too great. Figure 6 describes key indicators of the interested state.

Mindset	Key activity perception	Behavioral indicators	Thought indicators	Results
Interested	Important **YES** Meaningful **NO**	Comfortable with results Superficially enthusiastic Believes simplistic correlations Focuses on limiting risk	"I just have to do it." "Doing more is the key." "They can't fire me if I do the work." "This is a small part of my life." "I should."	Meets Expectations

Figure 6

SMALL WINS, BIG GAINS

Liz was the student teachers struggle to reach. She knew education was important enough to show up, but she didn't commit herself beyond the minimum required. By her senior year she had a reputation among faculty for being especially complacent — checked out.

Brett was new to the school and didn't know of Liz's previous reputation. When he looked over his roster for the incoming class her name registered no differently than any other. That would change when a colleague offered to help by reviewing the class enrollment with him.

"Go ahead and write her in for a 'C,'" was her dismissive recommendation when she got to Liz's name.

"No matter what effort you make that one will only do what it takes to survive."

Brett's first instinct was to heed his colleague's warning. But somehow that didn't seem right.

He was the younger of several brothers and thought of the challenges he faced for being branded for their actions.

He would approach Liz differently. And he hoped Liz would, in turn, approach herself differently.

When he walked in for the first day of class Brett only had names in his head — no photos to associate with them. About 15 minutes into the class a girl showed up and sat in the back of the room. After watching her through intermittent glances for the next 10 minutes it was clear that she was there to pass the time. Her materials were opened, but no notes were taken. She made only fleeting eye contact. She made little attempt to participate in discussions.

He knew it was Liz.

Breaking from the norm, he ended the lecture a few minutes early so he could talk with the class.

He wanted to paint for them a picture of what the class could be like for the rest of the year. He explained that he had no idea who they were, what previous reputations they may carry, or what kind of work they'd done before.

They had a blank slate.

He told them that he would trust their best efforts equally.

Then he did something they didn't see coming. He asked them to take a minute to draw a mental picture of how they wanted their lives to look in the year after graduation. He asked them if the dots connected between their current approach and what was in that mental picture.

He closed the class and didn't address the subject again.

This case would be fairy-tale like if Liz walked in the next day eager and radically changed. But that's not what happened. Instead, her emergence from interested was at first gradual, and then altogether.

It began with her listening more intently. Then there were at first small discussion contributions, growing in thoughtfulness over the weeks. As she gave, Brett increasingly called on her. The more stimulation she received, the more inquisitive and responsive she became.

About six weeks into the semester the colleague who'd warned Brett about Liz stopped him and asked if he'd noticed a difference in her. She said that Liz's younger brother was in her sophomore class and for the first time he was actively engaging the material. Brett shared that he'd seen a similar difference in Liz.

In addition to the final deliverable for that semester, Brett asked the students to write a letter to an upcoming senior and offer advice for their final year on the campus. He guided them to think of their own trajectory, and the inflexion points within it. Perhaps there were things that were especially helpful along the way or things they would do differently. Their only requirement was to be completely honest.

While educators tend to care deeply about the progress of their students, little could prepare Brett for what he read in Liz's letter. Tears, the combination of pride and genuine joy, marked his eyes as he worked his way down her paper.

The girl who cared just enough to survive — now cared deeply. She wrote profoundly, movingly about the moment when she decided to be more than a passive observer in her story. While her actions didn't change all at once because there were engrained habits and tendencies to work through, she gave them the chance to take root. And she soon flourished.

Her biggest mistake was not realizing this sooner. She described that this would have impacted who she surrounded herself with. She was always capable — but didn't always let that show. Brett didn't have contact with Liz until a few months later.

He and his wife were on a date to the movies when they realized the person taking their tickets was Liz. A wide smile came to the three as they exchanged pleasantries.

Liz couldn't hold back any longer. "I've been accepted to the graduate performing school of my dreams in New York!"

She looked the same, but somehow the pride beaming from her had transformed her. She emanated confidence.

Like the indifferent state, when recognizing complacency, the tendency is to respond with a strong-willed challenge. To compel action. But compelling and prompting look and are perceived very differently by the interested.

In Brett's awareness and to Liz's credit they got this formula right. Remember, the interested are showing up — they're just not tapping their real capabilities. More often this is because they see importance in doing the work (e.g. passing the class or keeping from getting fired), but they don't see value in giving of themselves meaningfully to it. Well-placed stimulation (one-part belief, one-part awakening) provides the difference.

The interested state needs a tangible reason, something it can clutch and hold onto, to take on the risk of doing something different than what is currently comfortable. It needs to see a positive, personal stake in the likely outcome. Then it needs to be fed.

The antidote to being interested isn't sweeping change. It is purposeful movements towards a specific, envisioned better outcome. It's planting the mental seed of a beneficial outcome and then experiencing success for putting some element of that thought to action. Momentum builds and the doing of one thing prompts the willingness to try others.

Decades of top-level research support this approach. Finding early roots in Emerson's social exchange theory and consistent validation through later studies, responses to stimuli can be predicted based on participant estimates of their approval and disapproval.[70][71][72][73][74][75]

People are more likely to break from an interested state if infused with belief that it's worth it to do so and then prompted to have a simple, direct experience to validate that belief.

Most, when honest, can think of personal experiences when this has been the case.

It's important to note that expectations imposed from the outside aren't nearly as meaningful as self-constructed ones. Moving from an interested to invested state stalls if powered alone by borrowed interest. Part of stimulation is providing a jump start, provoking meaningful thought, but ultimately, it's the owner who drives things forward.

Brett began by instilling belief — laying the foundation for others to open to a different possibility. Then he provided stimulation by asking the students to connect the dots between what they really cared about and their current approach. He was patient — letting Liz take part in forming what was meaningful to her. When she showed signs of emerging, he encouraged her. That was his genius. To have the intended effect he could only participate so much. While reliable principles helped to set the spark, it would only flame if it was unique to her.

---

70 Emerson, R. M. (1976). Social exchange theory. Annual review of sociology, 335-362.

71 Wayne, S. J., Shore, L. M., & Liden, R. C. (1997). Perceived organizational support and leader-member exchange: A social exchange perspective. Academy of Management journal, 40(1), 82-111.

72 Sanfey, A. G. (2007). Social decision-making: insights from game theory and neuroscience. Science, 318(5850), 598-602.

73 Gergen, K. (Ed.). (2012). Social exchange: Advances in theory and research. Springer Science & Business Media.

74 Cook, K. S., Cheshire, C., Rice, E. R., & Nakagawa, S. (2013). Social exchange theory. In Handbook of social psychology (pp. 61-88). Springer Netherlands.

75 Aryee, S., Walumbwa, F. O., Mondejar, R., & Chu, C. W. (2015). Accounting for the influence of overall justice on job performance: Integrating self-determination and social exchange theories. Journal of Management Studies,52(2), 231-252.

DISCOVERY SECTION

PART I: RESPOND

Respond to the questions below using the following rating scale:

A = Always. B = Often. C = Sometimes. D = Rarely. E = Never.

16. What percentage of your time tends to be spent in an indifferent state?

17. What percentage of your time tends to be spent in an interested state?

18. How often do you try to improve indifference or primarily through presenting a challenge?

PART II: DESCRIBE

For the following question, describe how you would most likely respond. To get the most from your efforts, don't describe what you think you should do, but rather what you would most likely do based on how you've responded to similar situations in the past.

You put a good amount of effort into something and receive well- reasoned feedback that doesn't meet with your expectations?

_____

_____

_____

_____

_____

_____

_____

_____

DISCOVERY SECTION

Consider the statement "Understanding expectation dynamics is vital to accurately recognize the lower levels of engagement. Rarely is indifference a function of DNA. More often it is a distorted or disproportionate view of circumstances. Instead of starting indifferent, people get there, often quickly, in response to negatively perceived unmet expectations" and detail a personalized experience with this principle.

PRACTICE ACTIVITIES SECTION

Compare two scenarios from your recent experiences in which you now recognize you were indifferent or interested. Presented with a similar situation, what could you do differently?

- Experience #1 — More Successful

- Experience #2 — Less Successful

DISCOVERY SECTION

Given a similar scenario going forward, how could you build from the more successful elements and improve on the less successful ones?

DISCOVERY SECTION

Describe a scenario in which someone close to you was indifferent. What signals did you notice in their action and communication? Then do the same for a interested.

- Indifferent

- Interested

DISCOVERY SECTION

Build a brief action plan for helping yourself and others emerge from indifference and complacency going forward.

- How will you detect and elevate from Indifference?

- How will you detect and elevate from Interested?

CHAPTER 7

TWO FEET

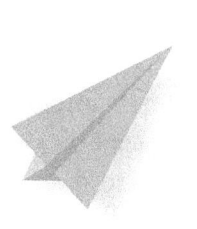

Raymond G. Ingalsbe was born in 1912 to unremarkable circumstances. His family owned a farm in rural New York where he worked before dropping out of high school and eventually enlisting in the U.S. army during WWII. Though a simple man, nothing about his life from that point forward was unexceptional. After completing basic training, Raymond was assigned to artillery and rose to the rank of Sargent. But his title tells little of the impact he had on his unit's men.

Sargent Ingalsbe was part of the allied Pacific landing in Okinawa under General Patton's command. Their assignment was to establish large caliber gun positions along the coastline to defend against bombing raids.

The task was tedious. The men had to dig large trenches to house the stationary guns. They had nothing but hand shovels to complete the job.

Reaching about three feet deep the men in Sargent Ingalsbe's unit stopped digging. They tried to persuade him that they had gone deep enough. He wasn't convinced. The men grew louder as they stood in the trenches — tired, exposed to the elements, sand sticking to their sweat-drenched bodies. Sargent Ingalsbe wouldn't relent.

"Two more feet."

The men kept digging. By mid-afternoon they had reached a depth of five feet.

"That should do it," Sargent Ingable thought.

The sound in the distance started as a low, rhythmic hum before converting to the thunderous roar unmistakable for early 20th century aircraft. Within seconds the silhouettes of incoming aircraft dotted the sky.

"Take cover!"

The nimble planes started high and then dived quickly as they marked their targets. Sitting like bullseyes within their newly formed trenches, a flood of 20mm munitions soon engulfed Sargent Ingalsbe and his men.

Every man would survive.

The angle of incoming fire had blasted through the top of the trenches and mainly hit at the 2 and 3-foot points in the back of the trench — leaving the unit just enough cover to duck below the incoming fire.

Two extra feet had saved the unit from something much worse.

Digging deeper wasn't by accident. Sargent Ingalsbe had a self-described deep love for his men. While untrained formally in geometry he knew he wanted to do everything in his power to keep them safe. This led him to carefully consider the likely trajectory of incoming planes. He also knew the size of his unit's 50 caliber guns and determined that a depth of about five feet would be needed. Though his only instructions were to dig trenches sufficient to house the large caliber gun defense positions, Sargent

Ingalsbe sensed that something more substantial was needed.

This was the first of several impressive events that would dot Raymond Ingalsbe's life until his death in 2012, just weeks short of his 100th birthday.

He returned from the war and took a job at GM as a steel press operator — responsible for folding metal into the under manifold for GM car heaters. Seeing Raymond's potential, his supervisor suggested that he take the GM Institute aptitude test.

Ingalsbe passed the test, rising to engineer and later executive with the firm.

Against the social pressure of his men to stop, what prompted Sargent Ingalsbe to dig two more feet — an act that would save them and shape the rest of his life?

Figure 7 includes the exact commendation Raymond Ingalsbe received from his commanding officer, John C. Hiles.

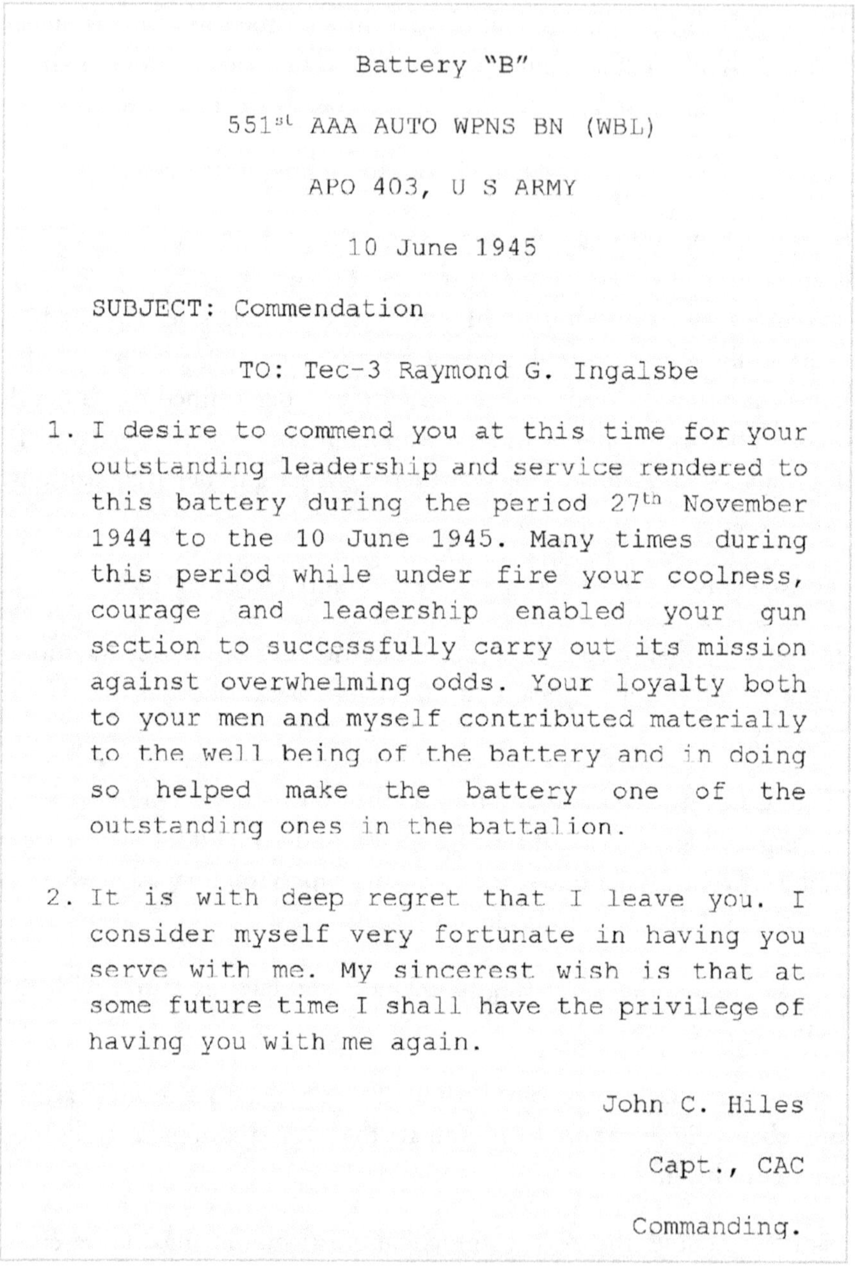

Battery "B"

551st AAA AUTO WPNS BN (WBL)

APO 403, U S ARMY

10 June 1945

SUBJECT: Commendation

TO: Tec-3 Raymond G. Ingalsbe

1. I desire to commend you at this time for your outstanding leadership and service rendered to this battery during the period 27th November 1944 to the 10 June 1945. Many times during this period while under fire your coolness, courage and leadership enabled your gun section to successfully carry out its mission against overwhelming odds. Your loyalty both to your men and myself contributed materially to the well being of the battery and in doing so helped make the battery one of the outstanding ones in the battalion.

2. It is with deep regret that I leave you. I consider myself very fortunate in having you serve with me. My sincerest wish is that at some future time I shall have the privilege of having you with me again.

John C. Hiles

Capt., CAC

Commanding.

Figure 7

INITIATIVE BEYOND INTEREST

A tipping point occurs between the interested and the invested mindset. Passive turns to active participating. The importance of getting things done is fueled by something more than obligation. Future interests inform present actions. You're no longer spectator to events, but a conscious agent within them.

Hidden camera social experiments highlight that what people do when others aren't watching, when the stakes seem low, or when stress is high often differs from what they think they'd do. One example is the 'person in need.' A community's population is sampled and asked how they would respond to a person falling down in front of them in need. The vast majority of respondents say they would stop and help. They project visionary behavior. Yet, when presented with similar events behind hidden camera only a small percentage offer aid. Pressed to explain why they didn't stop; the most common response is "what could I do?" Circumstance overpowers agency and the opportunity to shape one's environment is missed.

The interested state is primarily reactive — a function of situation rather than author of it. The invested state crosses the divide into proactive participation. Driven by the combined relevance of importance (something should get done) and meaningfulness (a deeper intent or personal meaning and relevance) it's when people effectively envision new outcomes and intentionally lay the groundwork for action.

Had Sargent Ingalsbe not given unique effort when ordered to dig gun positions his story could have died in that field. And the stories of his men. But he didn't want to just get the job done. Because of the affection he had for his men he wanted to do it well. He wasn't digging ditches to house guns; he was crafting shelters so his men could become fathers and grandfathers.

Research of high performers highlights the difference between interested and invested engagement. Take just one dimension of high performance — seeking new ideas — to see how the invested mindset works in practice.

Experiencing something is different than seeking new things. While billions of people around the world daily rise from bed, only some will actively look for new ideas. There are few genetic descriptions for this phenomenon. People who effectively do this come from varied demographics, levels of intelligence, and upbringing. What they do share is an acquired invested mindset — a belief that there is something new to discover and they are the ones to find it. This is demonstrated in their approach to daily observation.

There are three levels to observing the world around you. These levels share patterns with the indifferent, interested, and invested states. Think of them like digging through layers of soil before reaching pay dirt. High performers more often seek the cues that get at this deeper layer — where something unique can be found. This is not because they are simply more creative than others but because they effectively govern their approach to the world around them. Doing so requires moving from the indifferent (focusing on what's not possible) and interested (clinging to a present state) to a more invested mindset.

The surface level takes events on face value or focuses on what's not possible rather than what is. Like watching a television show in a desensitized or dogmatically skeptical state, you simply scan the environment without regard to understanding what may be causing events to unfold or the potential good to be found in them. Activities are completed without regard to greater quality. This approach almost never identifies new ideas. At the next layer, predetermined assumptions about what caused the events become your basis for interpreting them. You see something happen and quickly categorize and assign it merit based on your status quo. Almost without realizing it you filter out or discount what would require change or prompt improvement and magnify what does not. This leads you to project preconceived, maintaining, and deficit-oriented ideas onto the environment rather than allowing the environment to unveil new ones to you. Information is molded to match your existing circumstances. The danger is if all you see are more critical versions of what you already know and agree with then there's little room to consider new opportunities or improve quality.

This is the most common destination for observations and parallels the interested state. Those who remain at this layer may see new potential but they interpret it as uncharacteristic of and, therefore, inferior to or out of reach from what they already know. They focus on why something is illegitimate or won't work rather than envisioning the value of a new reality. Or they simply work through the task rather than considering how to improve its quality. This is especially prevalent when there is a politically, socially, or emotionally vested stake in the status quo — baiting one into a willingness to be wrong, to protect the self-belief of being right.

The core layer entails authentically considering the cues expressed in given scenarios without initially judging them. The intent is to genuinely understand and then to consider new potential in them. This does not have to take a lot of time, but it does require conscious effort. While engaging your environment, it can be easy to assume that what you observe is inferior to or incompatible with your prevailing ideals. These thoughts often manifest as defensiveness, dismissiveness, or derisiveness. Pushing past the two initial layers allows new ideas to surface because events, and their new potential, are interpreted in their true form with limited bias.

Consider the example of Howard Schultz of Starbucks who originally scouted the idea that transformed the firm while visiting espresso cafes in Milan.[76][77][78] The well-known story of the firm's founding too often overlooks the visionary element of Schultz taking to the streets of Italy to observe his new environment. Though his job was to attend a housewares show, like thousands before and after him, he wanted that business trip to produce something more.

So, he got outside his hotel. While walking the streets he noticed that coffee consumption in Milan looked different to back home. He could

---

76 Garthwaite, C., Busse, M., Brown, J., & Merkley, G. (2017). Starbucks: A story of growth. Kellogg School of Management Cases.
77 Schultz, H. (2012). Pour your heart into it: How Starbucks built a company one cup at a time. Hachette UK.
78 Koehn, N. F. (2001). Howard Schultz and Starbucks coffee company.

have determined that what he saw was uniquely Italian and wasn't applicable to other communities. He could have projected biases related to the amount of time that must be wasted as people interact in the cafes. He could have discounted his observations as inferior to prevailing business models in larger markets like the United States. Any one of these conclusions would have prompted him to dismiss what he observed as incompatible with his existing reality and derailed his ability to consider something new — just as hundreds of other coffee executives had done before him.

But he didn't. Instead, he paused and he watched. He listened. As verbal and non-verbal cues directed, he took note of the emotional satisfaction and value derived from embedding coffee into socially appealing activities — something completely foreign to the commodity model that then dominated the industry. This prompted him to dig deeper — to see what others missed. The result is one of the great stories of modern business.[79] [80] [81]

CEILINGS AND FLOORS

The *stick* and the *carrot* are commonly used metaphors for describing motivation — the stick rooted in fear and the carrot tied to hope. The stick approach seeks activity compliance by focusing on what will be lost. To retain one's job, for example, certain activities must be done. The belief is that compliance is unlikely without some form of coercion.

The carrot takes a different angle. In this approach expectations and incentives are the primary levers. Stretch objectives and concrete rewards replace coercion. Implicit to the carrot is that achievement is most likely through using positive incentives.

---

[79] Chuang, H. J. (2019). Starbucks in the World. HOLISTICA–Journal of Business and Public Administration, 10(3), 99-110.
[80] Rothaermel, F. T. (2017). Starbucks Corporation. McGraw Hill Education.
[81] Voigt, K. I., Buliga, O., & Michl, K. (2017). Globalizing Coffee Culture: The Case of Starbucks. In Business Model Pioneers (pp. 41-53). Springer, Cham.

These metaphors take on deeper meaning when comparing deficit and visionary thinking.

Deficit thinking is a primary theme in the indifferent and interested states. The focus is to avoid what could go wrong, maintain the status quo or minimum standard, or to cover up shortfalls. In contrast, the invested mindset benchmarks a starting point (like taking a vivid picture of a given situation) and then seeks to build from it — often in unique ways.

The example of a newly hired sales professional describes how this looks in practice. He was assigned a veteran mentor, with a reputation for candor, and the two went out to lunch within his first few days in his new position. The mentor didn't hold back, "I can tell you how to be the most successful person in this region." New to the position, the salesperson's interest peaked.

> "You need to understand your role better and get your brain in the right place."

Not what the junior hire expected to hear first so he was slow to respond. His mentor continued,

"How much money do you want to make in your first month in the field?"

"$5,000 gross commissions."

"Why'd you pick that number?"

"So, I can meet the standard to get to the next level of training,"

the junior salesperson answered. The company had a certain requirement within the first three months to continue in the position and qualify for the next step.

"Is that enough to feed your family?" the mentor continued. "What do you mean?"

"Does the company know how much you need to feed your family?" The question started to sink deeper.

The rookie explained that the net commissions that would result could not cover his bills, but he was also receiving a temporary salary.

> "Will you always receive that salary?" The mentor knew the answer but used the question to shape the rookie's thinking. "No. It goes away after a few months."

"You need to approach your work now like it doesn't exist."

The mentor prodded his trainee to describe minimum, medium, and maximum goals. He described the minimum standard as something that keeps the lights on at home and the maximum as something beyond your wildest dreams (something you'd "want to call home and tell your mom about" was his phrase). The rookie took the words to heart and over the next several days determined his first month's goals for those three ranges.

The rookie set his minimum goal at $8,000 in gross production, his midrange goal at $15,000 in gross production, and his maximum goal at $20,000. Armed with new mindset the rookie went to work. He reached $18,000 in gross commission (we worked closely with him and were able to directly verify these results).

Ecstatic, the rookie calls his mentor and tells him what he'd achieved.

> "Give yourself a quick pat on the back and get back to work for the next month."

> The rookie had hoped for more.

> "It's good to take a pause and appreciate what you've done, but don't stay in that place too long. My job isn't to help you to feel warm at night. We have to get you to be the highest performer in this region because that's your potential and that's what you told me you wanted."

The rookie didn't fully appreciate what his mentor had described and the next month he reached $7,000 in gross commissions. He described to us that he felt like a failure; he hadn't even come close to the previous month's production (remember, prior to meeting with his mentor his only goal was $5,000 gross commissions so he could qualify for the next stage of training). He called his mentor and told him he thought things weren't working they needed to try a different approach. He didn't like the sensation of underperforming his top-level goal by so much and thought it would be better to focus back down to the minimum and medium ranges so he could feel the satisfaction of meeting his goal.

> "Is the minimum standard really your goal? Feel free to lie to yourself if you want, but don't ask me to be part of it. I agree your goals need to be adjusted a bit. Up."

The rookie leaned forward in his desk towards the speaker phone he was using to make sure he'd heard correctly.

> "Take your average over the last two months and make that your new minimum standard. Stop basing your potential on somebody else's arbitrary numbers. That's what you already know you can do. Now let's stretch from here."

Though frank, he said it in a way that the rookie knew where he was coming from and latched on to the intent of his words. The new minimum goal was $12,000, mid-range was

$18,000, and maximum was $26,000. At $26,000 the net pay to the rookie would be approximately $10,000 — something his mentor told him he'd never seen done in a month in their first year.

The next month, his third in the field, the rookie did $32,000 in gross commissions

By the end of his first year the rookie had tallied $190,000 in gross commissions without inheriting any existing business (no standing book of business or wealthy relatives) or doing any different activities to win new clients than what the company had prescribed: phone calls, knocking on doors, and networking. But his results blew away those of others doing the same activities. At one point he was over 2000% the standard.

When asked what was different, he described,

> "My mindset was completely different, tapping into why my goals existed, and trying to make every contact the highest quality possible. That approach picked me up when I would have otherwise made excuses and focused me on shattering what wasn't previously considered possible. The funny thing is I didn't even see the results as extraordinary. They seemed natural — like I'd seen them before and was supposed to be performing at that level."

Think of the difference between the deficit and positive approaches in terms of their ceilings (what is considered possible) and floors (one's foundation or starting point).[82][83][84][85][86]

In deficit thinking the ceiling is hardcoded or fixed. The maximum it tends to consider is compliance to an average or fixed standard. The intent is to meet that line. But in a dynamic world rarely do outcomes perfectly match intentions. Because the deficit approach focuses on avoiding penalty or covering a shortfall or erring on the side of risk aversion when in a perceived leading position, minimum compliance is its upper limit. When that level is not met or a breakthrough doesn't occur, human tendency requires an explanation.

An outlet is needed — like water looking for the path of least resistance. Because something beyond the ceiling was considered infeasible or

---

82 Buxton, L. (2017). Ditching deficit thinking: Changing to a culture of high expectations. Issues in Educational Research, 27(2), 198.
83 Keefer, N. (2017). The Persistence of Deficit Thinking Among Social Studies Educators. Journal of Social Studies Education Research, 8(3), 50-75.
84 Seligman, M. E. (2019). Positive psychology: A personal history. Annual review of clinical psychology, 15, 1-23.
85 Compton, W. C., & Hoffman, E. (2019). Positive psychology. SAGE Publications.
86 Lopez, S. J., Pedrotti, J. T., & Snyder, C. R. (2018). Positive psychology: The scientific and practical explorations of human strengths. Sage Publications.

too difficult (or wasn't considered at all), the only place to turn for an explanation is the floor. The foundation starts to shift. Rationalization, justification, environmental blame, lowering expectations, or pretending not to really care in the first place take hold. Thoughts of: "It wasn't meant to be," "The system is flawed," "They don't get me," "If only the circumstances were different," "I'll just go somewhere else," "It wasn't that big of a deal anyway," "I've done all I could" flood in. Positive feelings like determination, refinement, anticipation, and clarity are crowded out by anger, pride, worry, and confusion.

With punctuation the metaphor, when mindset begins with an exclamation point or period (rather than a genuine question mark) and the ceiling is not met, you're prone to reinforce personal biases to insulate yourself from shortfall's realities or use externalities for excuses. Openness to new possibilities, genuine curiosity, situational and interpersonal empathy, and candid discovery suffer as a result.[87] [88]

A vicious cycle forms that further concretes the ceiling — and perforates the floor.

The positive approach has the opposite effect. The floor is hardcoded and the ceiling is perforated. This approach actively looks for greater good and allows space to exceed standard quotas. It takes a high-resolution image of one's starting foundation and seeks to build from its strengths or best parts in unique ways. Rather than staring laterally or at the floor, the invested mindset accepts and embraces one's starting foundation (wherever that might be–serving to concrete it) and then trains its attention on the possibilities beyond it.

The ceiling provides an initial goal or performance metric to orient activities. But because more than compliance is desired the ceiling is treated as a dotted line to be transcended. Compliance is achieved and, often, much more. Positive intelligence is a driving force; the focus is on what could be rather than what could not.

---

[87] Setti, R. (2019). Professional development: Mindset: How positive thinking boosts performance. LSJ: Law Society of NSW Journal, (52), 46.
[88] King, R. B. (2016). A fixed mindset leads to negative affect. Zeitschrift für psychologie.

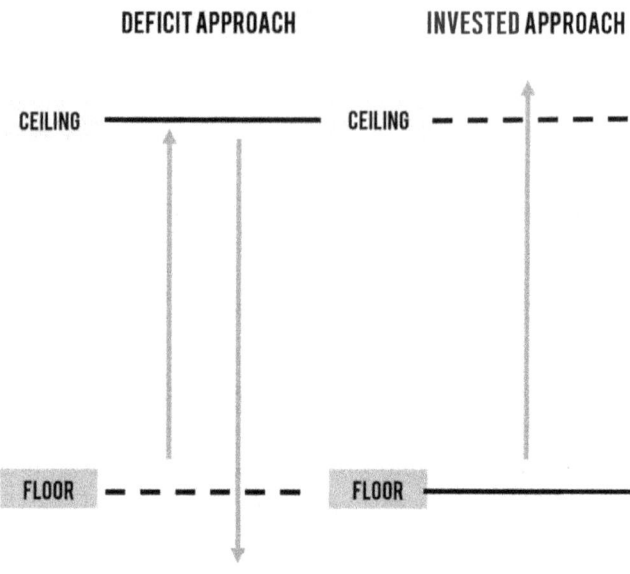

Figure 8

Over years of professional observation, this author's work has looked closely into the outcomes of deficit-oriented and visionary-oriented approaches. The first glance is misleading. Task completion rates are only moderately higher when anchored to hope rather than fear.

But that's the less valuable part of the story. The quality of how that task is completed (and related outcomes) significantly increases when driven by a invested approach. Checking the box as completed gives way to seeking new possibilities in what is done. Well-placed awareness and inquiry uncover new opportunities. Though both approaches complete things, the former is artificially capped at the minimum standard of what is expected. The invested mindset also meets that minimum standard, but it also has strong potential to break through that ceiling to improve on or exceed expectations.

This author's observations aren't alone. They share striking similarities to formal research about the impact of positivity on important measures like creativity, openness to change, satisfaction, and performance output.[89] [90] [91] [92] [93] [94]

From here it is easier to understand why some vision statements and visual prompts (motivational quotes, pictures, gestures, etc.) work and others don't. Symbolic interactionism (human understanding and actions are aided by symbols) has been formally studied for decades and used for much longer. [95] [96] [97] [98] [99]

It's not the statement alone that makes the difference — it's how it is perceived. Gestures, quotes, motivational speeches, or self-talk are just arbitrary words until the listener assigns them meaning. They need a personalized *why*; that effective emotional component that heightens senses and deepens interest in doing things well.

---

89 Imran, H., Arif, I., Cheema, S., & Azeem, M. (2014). Relationship between job satisfaction, job performance, attitude towards work, and organizational commitment. Entrepreneurship and innovation management journal, 2(2), 135-144.

90 Bono, J. E., Glomb, T. M., Shen, W., Kim, E., & Koch, A. J. (2013). Building positive resources: Effects of positive events and positive reflection on work stress and health. Academy of Management Journal, 56(6), 1601-1627.

91 Rego, A., Sousa, F., Marques, C., & Cunha, M. P. E. (2012). Optimism predicting employees' creativity: The mediating role of positive affect and the positivity ratio. European Journal of Work and Organizational Psychology,21(2), 244-270.

92 Avey, J. B., Luthans, F., & Youssef, C. M. (2010). The additive value of positive psychological capital in predicting work attitudes and behaviors.Journal of Management, 36(2), 430-452.

93 Avey, J. B., Wernsing, T. S., & Luthans, F. (2008). Can positive employees help positive organizational change? Impact of psychological capital and emotions on relevant attitudes and behaviors. The Journal of Applied Behavioral Science, 44(1), 48-70.

94 Luthans, F., Avolio, B. J., Avey, J. B., & Norman, S. M. (2007). Positive psychological capital: Measurement and relationship with performance and satisfaction. Personnel psychology, 60(3), 541-572.

95 Stryker, S. (1980). Symbolic interactionism: A social structural version. Benjamin-Cummings Publishing Company.

96 Solomon, M. R. (1983). The role of products as social stimuli: A symbolic interactionism perspective. Journal of Consumer research, 10(3), 319-329.

97 Blumer, H. (1980). Mead and Blumer: The convergent methodological perspectives of social behaviorism and symbolic interactionism. American Sociological Review, 409-419.

98 Blumer, H. (1986). Symbolic interactionism: Perspective and method. Univ of California Press.

99 Charon, J.M. (2009). Symbolic interactionism: An introduction, an interpretation, an integration. Pearson College Division.

This reaches back to classical thinker Socrates. One reason his approaches haven't been refuted is because they work. More directly, his method of asking tailored questions to prompt personal meaning and understanding was one of the first contributions to cultivating an invested mindset.

You can see how this works. When something is viewed as important there's an interest to get it done. Importance comes in a number of forms like rules, commands, obligation, and social pressures. However, importance tends to be superficial (outward facing) so it doesn't take root beyond what that external force requires.

When something is viewed as important and meaningful (useful; personally relevant) a different level of engagement results. Rote statements become personally tailored questions ("make 30 phone contacts a day" becomes "how can I best connect with 30 people today?"). Things that were overlooked are noticed. New potential is conceived. Opportunities that were discounted are more fully considered. Creativity replaces stagnation.

It works primarily because it doesn't dictate the source of meaning, but it does require that one be articulated (or several if applicable) and then linked to corresponding activities.

Because meaning varies from person to person projecting one note onto entire groups rarely works. For some the primary driver is the greater good. For others it is affiliation with a group or institution. Still others find deepest meaning in personal achievement and development. Even in large institutions, when done effectively all can tap their own source of meaning and maintain alignment to broader organizational goals.

What matters is that the meaning story is personalized and clearly articulated so that quality action follows.

Source of meaning relevance isn't trivial and is supported by behavioral science. An experiment using lottery design demonstrates the point. A room of people is equally divided into two groups and separated. Group one is assigned lottery tickets. The other group is told they can design their own ticket and select its number from the remaining sequence.

Each group is told that the true cost of the lottery ticket is one dollar ($1 USD).

Those in group one are approached and offered five dollars ($5 USD) to sell their tickets. It's a good offer and the majority take it.

Group two participants are approached with the same offer–

$5 for a lottery ticket with a $1 USD replacement value. Only a few take the offer. On average the others demand nearly 3x as much to sell their tickets.

Why?

The second group's behavior doesn't follow rational logic. Nothing about the probabilities changed. They stood no better chance of winning than the first group so their tickets weren't worth any more.

The only thing different was group two's personal investment in designing their own ticket. Because there is a piece of them wrapped up in the ticket, they assign it higher value.

Consider the experience of teaching young executives in Latin America.

During a breakout session to allow discussion of the Because I Will tool it was clear that one manager struggled to see her experience in the concept. She directed sales for her family's import/ export business. Her intelligence and talent were quickly evident. Her formal training was in a technical field and her interpersonal skills strong, so she'd assumed the sales role because that's where she was needed most.

The group was then asked to consider a professional activity they think is important. She wrote down "increase sales."

During the small group breakout, she was asked, "Why do you want to increase sales?"

"Because it's important."
"Why is it important?"

"Because then the family will thrive."

She then expressed that her work is interesting, but offered she was struggling to find new ways to grow the business.

"It's like I'm in a fog when I sit in my office and try to think about new sales. The ideas don't come naturally."

We continued to prod towards her meaningful why. "Why do you want your family to thrive?"

That question caused a pause. Not the type of casual pause when someone's thinking of a clever response. But the kind of pause that happens when everything slows down and you stop marking time. She was completely in the moment. By now the others in the group were captive; they were living the experience with her.

"For me family is everything."

Everyone felt the words as they came out. She spoke them almost reverently until she emphasized the last word everything.

The sensation was undeniable.

Overemphasizing the importance of increasing sales had robbed her of the meaning behind why she cared to do so. The pressure was tremendous. Staring at sales quotas made her resent them. She felt guilty for not being more creative. That pressure needed a release so she'd started to turn to the operating environment to justify the tepid growth.

"What if instead of repeating in your head over and over I've got to increase sales, which heightens anxiety, you began with a vision of the joy you feel around your family and how much they mean to you?"

The words quickly fell from her in a burst of inspiration.

"Because my family is everything to me, I'll help them increase sales."

"Lead with that mindset and let's see what you come up with."

Over the next ten minutes she developed more unique ideas than she'd done previously in the day. Her IQ hadn't changed. And she was equally ambitious before the breakout session. What changed was her mindset.

Equally vital, when she showed a hint of visionary behavior it was followed by the challenge to focus on the meaning she'd described and to act.

Another example from across the Atlantic demonstrates invested mindset in action. In the 1980's Tanzania, Africa was mired in one of the worst economic crises in its modern history. Political stability was suspect, inflation rampant, and the socialist economic experiment unraveling.[100] Within that context a young engineer needed to forge his path.

While formally trained in Europe as a Tanzanian national his goal was to return home and live a comfortable life in a state-owned firm. Within a few years he was comfortably positioned within a government organization as a respected engineer.

Then the bottom fell out of the economy.

His wage no longer livable the young man found himself at a crossroads. Around that time foreign aid organizations were ramping up activity in east Africa. This presented the option to seek entitlement funding, something many of his peers did in the absence of other ideas. He could try to move to another part of the world and apply his skills there. But aid felt like a bandage more than a solution and moving betrayed his deeper goal to help build his home country.

So, he stayed.

As a child he didn't picture life as an entrepreneur. But given this change in circumstances he saw entrepreneurship as the way to chart a new life. Without family resources or formal networks, he launched an IT firm. It was the only thing that didn't require a lot of start-up capital and he had at least cursory knowledge of the space.

---

100 Gray, H. (2018). Turbulence and order in economic development: Institutions and economic transformation in Tanzania and Vietnam. Oxford University Press.

At the time computers were illegal in Tanzania unless used by the government or organizations the government approved. For months and then years he was a small outfit determined to shape the environment on two fronts: change the way computing was regulated in the country and grow his business.

He succeeded on both fronts. Though not easy and requiring persistent effort he helped to change the perception of computing from an unknown entity to a tool for efficiency and progress. As regulation softened more firms could embrace these new technologies and his company was positioned to provide their IT services. Infotech Investment Group, LTD has since become one of the noted private companies in the region with interests in ICT, media, and telecom.[101]

Had he tucked away his meaning, his deeper purpose to help build his home country, and settled for a state of complacency it's hard to imagine any of this taking place. But he didn't. He realized that his capacity had less to do with the circumstances of his life and more to do with the focus of his life. Rather than resigning to perpetual aid recipient or mere consumer of things he became a contributor; a producer of things who actively shaped his circumstances.

Those with clear vision worry less about what isn't possible and focus more on pushing the limits of what is. They want to get things done and are willing to think of interesting ways to do them. Rather than self-stopping or passively mimicking the paths of others (assuming them to be right simply because they exist) they critically look to best practices (where possible) for insights or inspiration and determine their own course.

---

101 http://agln.aspeninstitute.org/profile/3376. Retrieved September 1, 2016.

POSITIVE INTELLIGENCE (PQ)

Positive intelligence is a widely studied theme. It is also a vital component of being invested. The results are compelling.

- In studies of more than 275,000 people, higher PQ leads to higher salary and greater success in marriage, work, sociability, health, friendship, and creativity.

- Higher-PQ workers take fewer sick days and are less likely to become burned out or quit.

- Project teams with higher-PQ managers perform 31% better on average when other factors are held constant.

- Higher-PQ workers deliver 37% higher sales, on average.

- Creativity output is 3x greater from Higher-PQ workers, on average.

- Higher PQ contributes to enhanced immune system functioning, lower levels of stress-related hormones, lower blood pressure, less pain, fewer colds, better sleep, and less likelihood to have hypertension, diabetes, or strokes.

Chamine, S. (2012). Positive intelligence: Why only 20% of teams and individuals achieve their true potential and how you can achieve yours. Greenleaf Book Group.

Lyubomirsky, S., King, L., & Diener, E. (2005). The benefits of frequent positive affect: does happiness lead to success?. Psychological bulletin,131(6), 803.

Figure 9

The challenge to find an activity's meaning, and one's role in facilitating that meaning, triggers a level of engagement unseen in the indifferent or interested states. Meaning gives purpose and clarity to activities. This provides courage to be honest, to be vulnerable, and to take on challenges. To consider what hasn't been done. The willingness to act in uncommon ways, and to be precise in those actions, results.

Training your mind on something you care about deeply, and then correlating needed activities to it, energizes the best parts of ingenuity.[102,103,104,105] It is not blind optimism. It's concerted effort to seize on new potential.

UNIQUENESS: INTRIGUING, BUT INCOMPLETE

Being visionary is an important step beyond merely interested. It invites the possibility of something more, something unique. But alone it's incomplete.

In business strategy circles there is a clear distinction between uniqueness and advantage. Uniqueness emphasizes doing things differently. The incentive is to change from doing one thing to another. But newness and value aren't the same thing. The former satisfies its own demands; its objective is met whenever something unique is done. The latter requires advantage to be created for the activity to be fully worthwhile.

History is littered with unique products and services and experiments that created little value. George Pullman's 19th century workers community is a good example. Pullman, a town established just south of Chicago, intended to be a utopian community where all workers' material and

---

102 Benkirane, O. (2019). Acting on purpose: the reflections of MIT student entrepreneurs (Doctoral dissertation, Massachusetts Institute of Technology).
103 Sternad, D., Kennelly, J. J., & Bradley, F. (2017). Digging deeper: How purpose-driven enterprises create real value. Routledge.
104 Cashman, K. (2017). Leadership from the inside out: Becoming a leader for life. Berrett-Koehler Publishers.
105 Creswell, J. D. (2017). Mindfulness interventions. Annual review of psychology, 68, 491-516.

spiritual needs would be met. Pullman placed himself as its leader and helped to oversee even the smallest details.[106] [107]

The idea was short lived. By 1894 the town's manufacturing profitability steeply declined. Pullman lowered wages and required workers to spend more hours in the factories, but didn't lower any of their living costs in the company owned town. Massive strikes ensued. One confrontation left 30 workers dead and the Supreme Court would shortly thereafter order the Pullman Company to divest itself of the town.[108] Rather than utopian life the Pullman experiment led to unnecessary casualties, heartache, and damaged social confidence. While incredibly visionary the idea created limited value and no true advantage.

The same principle exists in Shaper.

A visionary outlook needs to be paired with something else to maximize its effect. Without this match, it can mistake being different for invested.

INVESTED

Visionary is wanting to have a breakthrough. It's a shift — the desire to do something different than what is currently done. But different doesn't guarantee better. It's possible to be visionary without producing new value.

Invested engagement pairs desire with initiative. It is more likely to produce a breakthrough that centers on value and advantage.[109] While most advantages have an element of uniqueness, not everything that is unique creates advantage.

---

106 Buder, S. (1967). Pullman: an experiment in industrial order and community planning, 1880-1930. Oxford University Press.

107 Smith, C. (2007). Urban disorder and the shape of belief: the great Chicago fire, the Haymarket bomb, and the model town of Pullman. University of Chicago Press.

108 Klepper, Michael; Gunther, Michael (1996), The Wealthy 100: From Benjamin Franklin to John Gates—A Ranking of the Richest Americans, Past and Present, Secaucus, New Jersey: Carol Publishing Group.

109 Value and Advantage are understood to mean desirable and preferred.

The invested mindset is the top level of engagement (Level 3). In this state visionary sparks are built upon and refined. Trade-offs are successfully managed; the ideas and activities that create the strongest advantages are embraced and lesser things are discarded. Agent thinking and actions is fully embraced; you want the opportunity and responsibility to account for your ideas and efforts. What emerges is advanced (creates value; is desirable) and original (relevant; not a copy or imitation; something that improves quality from a previous approach).

The example of an American college football team shows how this can work. In the mid-1970's the sport was dominated by powerful running attacks. Strategy on the offensive side of the ball looked similar across the country and the teams with the most athletic running backs and best offensive linemen typically won. Universities outside the natural footprint of where the best athletes resided were disadvantaged.

One coach took an innovative approach and is largely credited with pioneering the forward pass in the collegiate game. He knew his players weren't as big or fast as other teams (nor would they be anytime soon). And his school's location and composition were unlikely to consistently attract the country's best athletes. But rather than deride the system, grow frustrated with his circumstances, or submit to mediocrity he took a compelling turn to his situation. He asked what his players could do well — perhaps even better than others. He looked for what was compelling about what they had access to. The players on his team were smart, disciplined, and willing to stand out from others. They wouldn't be threatened by a new approach to the game. They would embrace it.

Armed with that spark he considered ways to accentuate his players' strengths and neutralize opposing teams. He looked for soft spots — ways he could approach other teams that would create an advantage. A headful of ideas flooded in. He worked through these ideas until the most advanced and original approach rose to the top.

His persistence paid off. The team would focus on passing while other teams were built to run the ball and to stop the run.

Their passing attack would be based on precision routes and timing to negate their opponents' athletic superiority.

Soon the team was forward passing as much as they ran the ball. Within fifteen years the school won a national championship and produced winners of the game's most prestigious offensive awards (including the Tommy O'Brien Award and Heisman Trophy).

When asked by a former player, himself taking over an underperforming program, how his coach was able to turn the page on the school's decades of losing he replied directly,

> "We quit worrying about what we didn't have and started focusing on what we did."[110]

There are a lot of different things the coach could have done. He could have tried new ways to recruit better running backs. Or he could have devised different running plays. His background was in the running game and most of his experience wanted to steer him in that direction. But that wouldn't have created the advantage they found in the forward pass.

Revisiting the example of Howard Schultz in Milan, his willingness to look for new ideas by walking the streets of that city was visionary. Considering the potential in something different was a necessary step. But that alone wasn't enough. What happened next is what tipped the scale.

He worked through his observations and dug deeper — to see value that others missed in the then commodity-driven industry. He stepped into the invested mindset by considering how to effectively make socially-rich, quality product experiences available globally. He couldn't just imitate what he saw. The approach would need to be modified to scale profitably — while retaining the essence of social vibrancy. The idea to have an idea was invested. It was invested to refine the idea until its true advantage was found — and then to act on it.

---

110 http://www.deseretnews.com/article/865648863/QA-with-Ty-Detmer-Talking- about-the-past-present-and-future-of-BYU-football.html?pg=all. Retrieved March 1, 2016.

The invested mindset accepts the challenge to ask "What valuable thing isn't being done as well as possible? Or "How can I make what I'm tasked with more valuable?" Being visionary opens your line of sight to new possibilities and anchors the search to the deeper meaning of why you engage in the activities. Then the invested refines that headful of ideas to pinpoint the advantage.

What emerges tends to avoid the copy of a copy trap. It's original to you–and advanced. It creates true value.

INVESTED MINDSET (LEVEL 3) EARLY SIGNALS:

- **Seeks opportunity to discover,** What valuable thing isn't being done as well as possible?

- **Takes the initiative to advance,** How can I make what I'm tasked with more valuable?

- **Views accountability as beneficial,** How can I best account for my actions – and encourage the same in others?

The invested state can be found in all walks of life. It can be observed in remote villages in developing nations, in executive teams of global companies, in elite graduate school classrooms, or as parents and children interact. And this author experienced this first hand when the organization of a renowned South American chef reached out to help them analyze ways to align rural farming techniques with international standards so the restaurant group could source more from indigenous providers.

Gaston Acurio was not groomed to be a chef. The son of a career politician, Acurio studied law and it was thought that he'd follow his father into politics. Then something changed.[111]

---

111 http://www.gastroenophile.com/2013/03/interview-with-perus-gaston- acurio-by.html Retrieved September 1, 2016.

Mindset	Key activity perception	Behavioral indicators	Thought indicators	Results
Invested	Important **YES** Meaningful **YES**	Mainly driven by Hope or Generosity Resilient to rejection Feels connected to the *why* Sees risk as positive and necessary Seeks competitive advantage Doesn't confuse different and better – seeks to create greater value	"I love what I do." "I'm very grateful." "How can this be even better?" "I want to share what has helped me." "How can this be more valuable?" "Let's make this a reality"	Outstanding

Figure 10

The path to politics was well-defined, but it felt forced. He had an artistic inner-voice that grew loud the closer he got to passively sliding into his father's footsteps.

So, he took the visionary step and enrolled at Le Cordon Bleu in Paris. Before the age of 45 he would become the most renowned chef in his home country of Peru.

While going to culinary school was visionary, it's what he did with the opportunity that qualifies as invested.

Once back in Peru he took a series of jobs in other chefs' kitchens honing his skills and sharpening his ideas. During that time, he carefully observed the gaps in local offerings and determined that Peru had a wealth of quality ingredients and traditions that hadn't yet been elevated to fine dining standards. Then he launched his own restaurant (together with his wife, Astrid, whom he met in culinary school). Today Acurio's franchise empire spans Latin America and has inspired other chefs in the region to re-envision their own local cuisines.

Acurio's thirst for creating new value didn't wane with his increased success. It was this commitment to bring elegance to traditional Peruvian ingredients — to push the boundaries of what's possible and then to turn that idea to reality — that prompted Acurio's organization to engage the advisory team for help to extend their supplier network to indigenous farmers in the Andes highlands. Known for deeply flavored and colorful produce, Acurio accurately understood that if these farmers could be groomed to meet urban code requirements their standard of living would rise and Acurio's restaurants could feature some of the country's finest produce — and the impactful story of its growers.

Acurio's consistently invested approach had led him to another worthwhile advantage.

Figure 11 - Exterior photo of Astid y Gaston from 2015.

DISCOVERY SECTION

PART I: RESPOND

Respond to the questions below using the following rating scale:

A = Always. B = Often. C = Sometimes. D = Rarely. E = Never.

19. What percentage of your time tends to be spent being visionary?

20. What percentage of your time tends to be spent in an invested state?

21. How often do you skillfully encourage others to be invested?

PART II: DESCRIBE

For the following prompt, describe how you would most likely respond. To get the most from your efforts, **don't** describe what you *think you should do*, but rather *what you would most likely do* based on how you've responded to similar situations in the past.

You think you have a good idea and believe it could be important to others.

Consider the statement "Visionary is wanting to have a breakthrough. It's a shift — the desire to do something different than what is currently done. Competitive uniqueness is the target. But different doesn't guarantee better. It's possible to be visionary without producing new value. Invested is having a breakthrough that centers on value and advantage" and outline examples of when you've been visionary and when you've been invested.

PRACTICE ACTIVITIES SECTION

Compare two scenarios from your recent experiences in which you now recognize you were interested or invested. What was the difference between the two?

- Experience #1–Interested

- Experience #2–Invested

- What explains the difference?

DISCOVERY SECTION

Given a similar scenario going forward, how could you build from the more successful elements and improve on the less successful ones?

CHAPTER 8

BUILD **CONGRUENCE**

The scene is a West African conference room. Filled to capacity, attendees had traveled from nearly a dozen neighboring countries for the multi-day event. Thousands of hopeful participants submitted applications to receive the advanced training they expected would help to take their young businesses to a new level. An energy buzzed in the room as those selected waited for the session to begin.

Then it happened. The organizers realized that three primary languages were spoken among the group and there were translators for only two of them.

Professional trouble-shooting quickly devolved into something more chaotic. Organizers darted in and out of the room hoping to find the missing translator. Attendees realized what was happening and began to stir and then to voice displeasure — in their primary language. Other options exhausted, the organizers were forced to move forward with the limited translation service. Nearly half of the participants, some who'd traveled close to twenty hours by road to attend, understood little of what was taught.

Imagine trying to convey high-level concepts to portions of an audience that speak a different language — with no translation in between. Now consider being on the receiving end of messages communicated in a different language than what you understand. Whether internally or interpersonally, it's vital to identify the levels of engagement and employ strategies that target their primary needs to unlock their best parts.

FLUIDITY

Have you noticed that certain levels of engagement resonate differently for you at different times? Perhaps this happened while reading previous chapters. Congruence (state of corresponding) helps to explain why.

Human experience is dynamic. And human response to that experience can also be dynamic. Engagement occurs on a continuum — ranging from indifferent at the lower end to invested at the top end. Because no one stays in one state indefinitely (and can simultaneously be invested in one aspect of life and indifferent in another) without effort, and each state is sensitive to upward or downward movement based on certain inputs, each level requires a different strategy to unlock its best parts.

This came into focus when we presented to managers from leading industrial and construction companies in Phoenix, Arizona. At one point attendees were broken up into partnerships to work on influencing someone in an indifferent state — alternating roles so that each person could experience being the manager and the recipient.

During the report out afterwards, we asked participants to describe their impressions. A man we estimated to be in his thirties raised his hand. He worked for one of the largest plumbing companies in the state and was helping them to expand to other states. He seemed very capable — and busy.

He mentioned that he really struggled with the activity. We asked what made it hard and he said that when serving the role of the indifferent person and being told he was valued, a strategy targeting the indifferent person's primary need, he felt uncomfortable and even awkward.

Then something happened as he continued to discuss his experience. It was as if he was having two conversations at the same time — one expressed in the words he shared with the group and another internally as he seemed to process what he was describing at a deeper level.

"I get it."

His words were a bit abrupt so it took time for those around him to understand what he meant.

Like he'd just found something and wanted to share how he'd done it, he went on to describe that even though he tried for the simulation's sake — he couldn't really fake his engagement state. He was in an invested place and the words being expressed to him seemed completely misfit. Because he wasn't indifferent the words coming from the person he was paired with felt disingenuous and strange.

He went on to describe that the reason he didn't feel comfortable was because the strategy being used was incongruent with his engagement state.

"This happens all the time with the people I manage. I'm in one place. They're in another. But I've never thought about congruence and I never tailor the message to meet someone's engagement state."

Like many, this gentleman presented as intelligent and ambitious. But by failing to appreciate congruence he'd struggled to have the desired impact. He realized when expressing 'I get it' that by approaching each state strategically the odds of a positive effect improve. Think of this as activating the brain in the way it is best prepared to process and elevate from a given state. Just as it doesn't make sense to play one set of notes for different songs, it doesn't make sense to treat different engagement states, each with unique primary needs, the same way.

PRIMARY NEEDS

Farms can be fertile ground for more than crops. That was the case in rural Idaho when the son of a potato farmer caused tremendous damage to a piece of machinery that could have been avoided.

Like most family operations, this teenager was expected to contribute to daily choirs during the summer. The day of the disaster began like most. He was up before sunrise and assumed a familiar position in the driver's seat of the massive harvester. It ended with him learning about much more than a paycheck.

Each weekday the boy's routine was similar. Wake up. Quickly force down some food. Throw on his headphones and fire up the combine. He would then go about his work without thinking much about what he was doing.

This day was no different until about an hour into his shift — when smoke started billowing out of the combine. Then the engine seized.

The boy's heart sank. He fumbled around for several minutes to see if he could come up with a quick fix. He couldn't.

Out of options, he left the combine in the field and went to get his father. After exhausting everything his father could think of, they called for a mechanic. The mechanic stripped the machine enough to inspect the motor.

He was shocked by what he found.

The side of the engine block had a hole in it. Analyzing the cause deeper, the mechanic explained that the arm connected to one of the pistons had a broken coupling ('keeper' as he called it) that caused the arm to come apart and repeatedly hit the side of the engine block until it punched a hole. At the time a coupling for the arm cost about 20 cents USD.

The punctured engine block and extensive labor to fix it cost nearly $20,000.

Knowing the considerable and continuous noise the arm pounding against the engine block would have made, the mechanic was baffled and struggled to deliver the news to the farmer and his son. He first stared at his shoes and shook his head before coming up with the words to tell them the extent of the damage. Then he looked up at the boy, genuinely curious, and asked,

"What I want to know is how you didn't hear it?"

The sound of a piston arm puncturing the side of the engine block should have been suspicious — if not alarming. Anyone paying reasonable attention would have quickly heard the thunderous banging and could have stopped the combine before it suffered further damage.

The boy never considered listening for something incongruent to how he thought the machine should sound and work. So, he just continued down the same path. And by numbingly plowing through the task he didn't give space to consider how to do it well. The result was watching his father struggle for months to pay for the damage to the farm's most important piece of equipment.

Each level of engagement gives off certain cues that are grounded in certain needs. Think of each level as its own language. When these needs are accurately identified and paired with strategic thought patterns crafted for that level an effective Shaper cycle triggers. Congruence is detecting and listening to these cues and then efficiently engaging them to unlock their best parts and elevate towards the invested.

Whether individually or interpersonally the process is similar. Effective Shaping occurs when a present state is listened for, accurately identified, its corresponding needs are understood, and specific strategies are employed to unlock its best parts. While people are unique, engagement states share prevailing tendencies related to mindset patterns. These unifying links are common across the human experience — allowing for a repeatable approach.

INDIFFERENT

Think of a time when you were genuinely out of sync, disengaged. You struggled to see the importance or meaning in something you were tasked with doing. The activity felt like going through the motions and, if done, was given the minimum effort required. Perhaps it was a course in school or an assignment at work. Maybe your mind goes to a certain event at home.

What did you really need in that moment?

Primary symptoms of indifferentness are under-caring and under-producing. In practice it looks like underperforming talent, underwhelming interest, or undiscovered potential. Controlling for adequate knowledge and skill to complete given activities, beneath the surface indifferentness is rooted in the lack of *belief* that something (or someone) is worth it. Across time *belief* has been among the most resiliently used words in the English language — underscoring the human desire for connection.

Two friends built homes next to each other at nearly the same time. In several cases they used the same sub-contractors for various parts of the work. One home has limited to no cracks to the foundation. The other home has experienced extensive cracks needing repair.

In the building process all activities are inter-linked. Doing one thing well provides the potential for another thing to go well. But getting a substantial item wrong impacts everything that comes after. One of the most important, and underappreciated, activities is something no one sees after the home is built — dirt compaction prior to laying the foundation.

Done near flawlessly, the concrete foundation rests on firm footing with little risk of shifting or settling. Anything less puts the foundation at risk once the weight of the rest of the home and the moving soil underneath take effect.

The same contractor did the compaction work for both of our friends' homes side-by-side to each other, using the same equipment, employing a similar contract, under the same state regulation to achieve at least 90% compaction. While the regulation standard was met in both cases the contractor's perceived commitment to one of the homeowners was different. This homeowner was building his first custom home. He wanted it to be his last. Prior to the contractor starting the job the homeowner asked if he could have a few minutes and explained something similar to,

> "I've never built a custom home before. I've done as much homework on this as I can think to do, but I realize you know much more about it than me. I've spent the last decade living in an under-sized home with a growing family saving money to be able to afford this house. It's where my extended family will gather. We hope to never move. We want our grandchildren to play in the backyard their parents did. It means everything to us."

The contractor, appreciating the sacrifice the homeowner had made and the meaning attached to the house, instantly elevated his mental commitment and responded,

"I will make sure you never have a problem with this foundation."

Without strong compaction work the rest of the home would have suffered. But by laying the quality foundation from the onset the rest of the home could come together equally well.

Indifferentness directly relates to lacking belief in the worthwhileness of a particular activity, those involved in it, or those impacted by it. On the surface it looks like mindlessly going through the motions. A home built on top of it will likely experience foundational cracks and need to be rebuilt or risk catastrophe.

This is where congruence comes into play. When observing the indifferent state, a first reaction can be to lob challenges at it (e.g. equivalent to throwing up the house on top of it). Because the mindset in the indifferent state already lacks belief, however, challenges tend to reinforce that disbelief.

Decades of social and cognitive science describe that humans can self-regulate; and the capacity and willingness to do so relates to the attitude and intentions associated with the behavior.[112] [113] [114] [115] [116] [117] The difference between the compaction results for one of the one homebuilder compared to the other had nothing to do with different skills or resources or environments. It had much to do with the mindset of the contractor when engaging the work.

---

112 Ajzen, I., & Fishbein, M. (1980). Understanding attitudes and predicting social behaviour.

113 Ajzen, I. (1991). The theory of planned behavior. Organizational behavior and human decision processes, 50(2), 179-211.

114 Bandura, A. (1991). Social cognitive theory of self-regulation. Organizational behavior and human decision processes, 50(2), 248-287.

115 Conner, M., & Armitage, C. J. (1998). Extending the theory of planned behavior: A review and avenues for further research. Journal of applied social psychology, 28(15), 1429-1464.

116 Hofmann, W., Schmeichel, B. J., & Baddeley, A. D. (2012). Executive functions and self-regulation. Trends in cognitive sciences, 16(3), 174-180.

117 Burnette, J. L., O'Boyle, E. H., VanEpps, E. M., Pollack, J. M., & Finkel, E. J. (2013). Mind-sets matter: A meta-analytic review of implicit theories and self- regulation. Psychological Bulletin, 139(3), 655.

Believing that what is done matters and that others value it releases an effect that raises output quality beyond what is otherwise produced. So, when recognizing that you or someone else is in an indifferent state congruence requires understanding the primary needs (value and belief) and matching your input to those needs.

INTERESTED

At a networking dinner event between financial fund representatives and financial planners the following exchange took place. A fund representative approached an up-and-coming planner and early in the conversation asked,

"How do you want us to interact with you to retain your business?"

On the surface the question seems reasonably tailored — something that could easily come from a sales seminar. The planner's response showed the holes in the approach.

"Instead of asking *how*, I'd rather you start by considering *if* we'd like to be contacted."

The planner wasn't trying to cause offense. The response given, however, pointed to the underlying connection between the representative's approach and the interested state. Complacency is built on assumptions rooted in previous experiences, obligation, and one's risk relationship. It appreciates that certain things are important but stops short at connecting that importance to a deeper purpose. And it tends to seek the path of least resistance by adding to what is currently done rather than stepping back and considering how something is best done.

Because interested behavior tends to approach or meet expectations it can have a blinding effect to greater potential. In practice, it lacks awareness and primarily seeks to retain one's position within what is already comfortable. Viewed through this lens the representative didn't really want to learn about or understand the planner. He simply wanted to figure out the easiest way to retain a decent level of business.

The inflection point (moment when something improves or declines) for complacency is learning interest. Unchecked, new approaches and information are largely deflected because they represent a shift from what is presently familiar or convenient. The primary need to elevate the interested state is stimulation — seeking the meaning in what is done and having validating experiences with improved or alternative ways to do them.

You can see how this plays out in all kinds of settings. It's the dad who's put in a solid day at work and then snaps at the kids who anxiously ask him to play with them when he walks in the door. It's the doctor who tells her staff never to book more than a certain number of patients in a day rather than sitting down with them to consider better ways to serve more people. In both scenarios the message conveyed is interested-state conformity; the recipient feels misunderstood and under appreciated and the giver feels frustrated that new alternatives are so easily deflected.

Congruent to elevating the interested state is to stimulate a learning experience grounded in an activity's underlying purpose — then making a commitment to act on it (or inviting another to do the same if dealing interpersonally). Prior to walking in the door, the father would take five seconds to pause, consider what his kids might be thinking about and what a meaningful interaction would do for them (even if brief), and then walk in the door and give action to his thoughts.

INVESTED

Invested is when the exuberance and creativity of the visionary combines with strategic intelligence and resilience to unpack true value and see it through to effective implementation – it's the initiative to follow through on what matters most. This mindset is marked by consistently seeking the best things to be done, in the best ways, and showing persistence in the face of adversity and unfounded rejection. The invested mindset conveys comfort with questions and challenges, and discomfort with mediocrity. This state seeks ways to reach and attract feedback from those competent in the subject at hand.

Observed across a variety of personality profiles the invested state is distinguished by a willingness to see beyond simplistic surface events and commit the effort to grasp underlying conditions – to convert positive intentions to practical initiative.

It approaches situations with pauses and questions (rather than pre-formulated responses) to isolate the best alternative. It is willing to stand alone and be different, but does so intentionally with an eye toward value creation rather than treating difference as an end in itself.

History often celebrates the outcomes of the invested actor without doing justice by the process. Throughout time the mindset effect has shown to be fundamental to what would follow. The study of Edison, Franklin, Da Vinci, Bell, Galileo, Curie, Fleming, and Feynman (to name a few) all weave narratives of significant mental fortitude prior to experiencing tangible breakthroughs (and during the adoption phase) when previous conceptions fought to stamp out new alternatives. In their experiences the invested mindset's resilience in the face of adversity is highlighted; not in a dogmatic or sheltered way but by constantly seeking the better alternative in any circumstance. While commitment (indicative of invested) shares some characteristics with stubbornness (indicative of interested), it is differentiated by its learning orientation. The former consistently probes for improvement and is persistent within what is found while the latter walls itself off to new alternatives.

Trade-offs between good and exceptional (distinguished by the predicted value created) are more comfortable to the invested mindset. Going through revisions to isolate the most essential parts of something is viewed positively; a step closer to refinement.

At this level the interested's willingness to side-step passive mimicry is given a final layer of sophistication: the drive to push new alternatives to their most elegant form. Neither simplistic nor overly complex will do. The interest is to *get it right*. Its congruence catalyst is challenge in the form of polish input and a call for initiative and quality action.

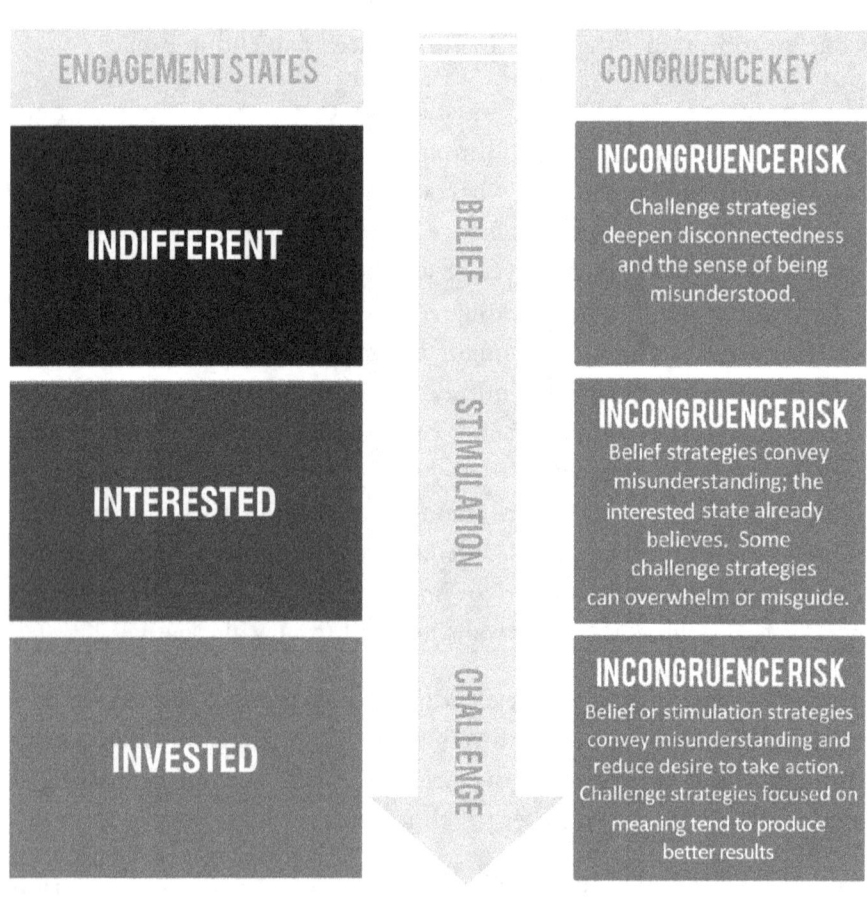

Figure 12

STATEMENTS AND STRATEGIES

Mindset is thought-driven so Shaper statements carry considerable weight. It is also the epicenter of performance and the catalyst to emotional attitude and related results. When statements and strategies are anchored to the primary needs of a particular state an elevating effect tends to take place. What was indifferent can become invested through this pattern.

Human experience is largely comprised of two themes: beliefs (patterns of thought) and behaviors. When people's behaviors don't match up with their beliefs, they find themselves at a crossroads. If they like their behaviors enough they'll try to change their beliefs to support them. But shaping thoughts to behaviors is largely reactive (compared to the proactive Shaper of thoughts that inform behaviors). Like binging on candy to drive down hunger this can feel initially satisfying — but it's neither substantial nor sustainable. Significant cognitive dissonance can result.[118][119][120][121]

Congruence is the straightforward call to recognize this ordering and to work effectively within it. Contextual perception is the mandate. By understanding a current level of engagement and targeting to its primary elevating needs both the belief (way of thinking) and the behavior are positively affected.

Just as the capable physician aptly diagnoses symptoms (or cues) and tailors the prescription — so it is with congruence to the Shaper cycle. Flu medication is ill-fitted for a broken bone and the human condition

---

118 Festinger, L. (1962). A theory of cognitive dissonance (Vol. 2). Stanford university press.
119 Elliot, A. J., & Devine, P. G. (1994). On the motivational nature of cognitive dissonance: Dissonance as psychological discomfort. Journal of personality and social psychology, 67(3), 382.
120 Harmon-Jones, E., Harmon-Jones, C., & Levy, N. (2015). An action-based model of cognitive-dissonance processes. Current Directions in Psychological Science, 24(3), 184-189.
121 Hinojosa, A. S., Gardner, W. L., Walker, H. J., Cogliser, C., & Gullifor, D. (2016). A Review of Cognitive Dissonance Theory in Management Research Opportunities for Further Development. Journal of Management, 0149206316668236.

is more responsive to statements and strategies that are suited for the primary needs of a given state.

Consider three sequences to see how this works.

INDIFFERENT TO INTERESTED

It is not uncommon when giving a presentation or speech to focus more on developing interesting content than being genuinely interested in the audience's needs. The first step to counter this tendency is to ask, "Where are these people?"

From this question you recognize the prevailing mindset is indifference, for example. You understand this to mean their primary elevating needs are rooted in seeing importance and meaning in who they are and what they do. They need to feel valued. When addressing them you describe how worthwhile they are and express gratitude for the positive qualities they exhibit. You avoid the tendency to inundate them with challenges (which activate defensive tendencies in the indifferent state) and instead infuse them with a sense that what they do has importance and is worth it.

Reactions convey the impression that 'someone gets them.' Their next step is likely to be far more productive.

INTERESTED TO INVESTED

Ten years into your career you've grown comfortable. You know how to get the returns needed to meet expectations. You are superficially enthusiastic, but internally indifferent. This gap is growing and you want to stem the tide.

Strategies focused on personal worth, while appreciated, do little to positively catalyze your approach. The primary elevating need is stimulus to find and attach deeper meaning to what you do and then to validate the process through initial actions in that direction. You look to the

Because I will model found in Chapter 3 to identify an initial spark. It prompts you to be authentic about the substantive *why* within your activities.

You recognize that size and speed matter. With that spark you isolate an initial way to reimagine the underlying intentions to your work so you can have a positive experience with considering new alternatives. This fuels the best parts of the state and point it in the direction of visionary. The sensation of learning and developing begins to rekindle deeper interest — personally and as you consider the potential to your contributions — leading to new idea generation and isolating opportunities for improvement. While these inputs can happen in rapid lock-step, their ordering matters.

The congruent approach is to present supportive challenges that intelligently sift through the advantage (value creation) in various ideas and activities. It is the prompt to realize that uniqueness alone isn't an advantage — but rather advantage contributes to uniqueness. A refining process ensues that gives substance and form and value to otherwise abstract concepts. Visionary and invested work together in that visionary reinforces the meaning and catalyzes learning interest. Invested builds on the meaning and refines it to produce value. What results is something far more grounded and elegant.

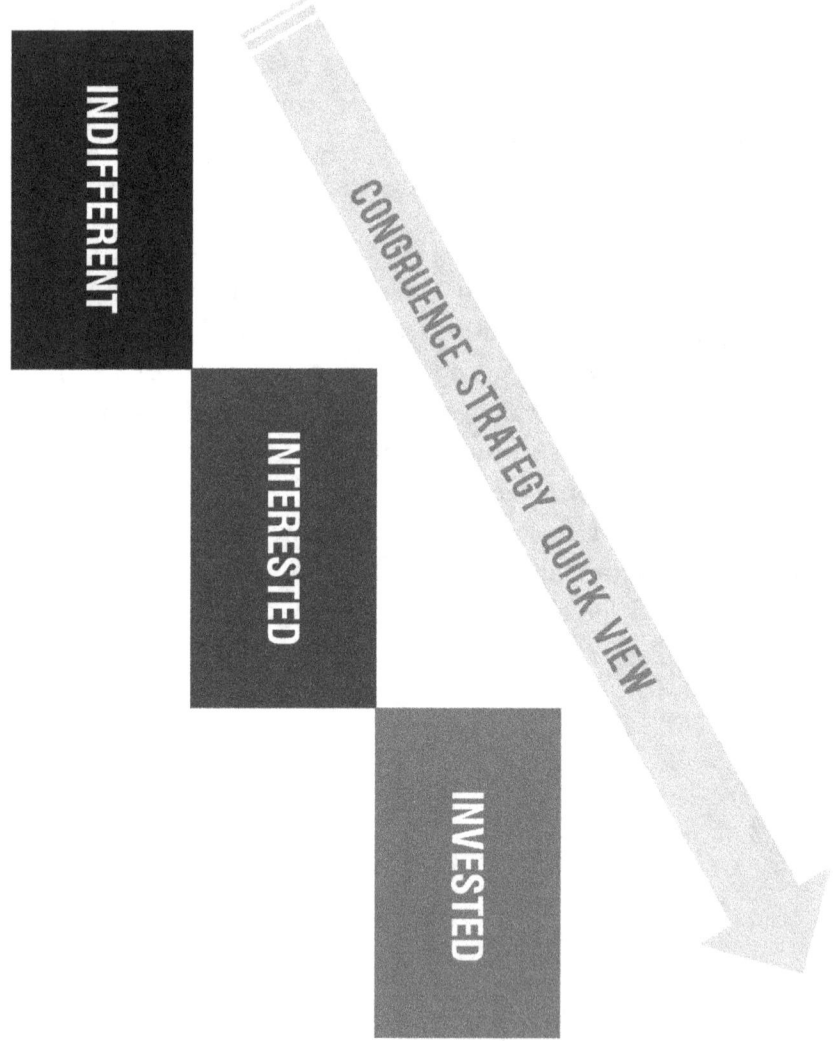

Figure 13

IN ACTION

When interactions, either individual or interpersonal, begin with 'What is my (or their) mindset right now?' the opportunity for an elevating effect presents. Rather than beginning with a period or, worse, exclamation point — an intentional question invites a range of positive options. This initiating question prompts you to think about what you (and others) think about. Congruence is then possible, which increases the odds of igniting the Shaper cycle in predictable, positive ways.

This was reinforced during several engagements with a regional healthcare company. The marketing director was incredibly dynamic and consistently operated in an invested state. The doctors who actually saw the patients felt overworked. During one interaction we listened to the marketing director bound into the hallway between patient visits and explain to one of the doctors how a new initiative would generate up to 20% more patients. Knowing the potential income boost to the doctor she expected to be heaped with praise. What she received was a blank stare and then a series of descriptions about how they couldn't absorb that much growth. He then went into the next operatory and she was left frustrated that he hadn't appreciated what she'd done.

Incongruence in that exchange was glaring — from both sides. When studying the company deeper it was apparent that this was not an isolated event. Intangible but clear lines were forming between those who wanted to grow and those who did not or could not see how it was possible within their current resource composition.

The marketing director, whose contribution was measured by new revenue generated, struggled to reconcile how anyone could react negatively to what she'd done. The doctor, who felt maxed out and described consistently being approached with such ideas without context or understanding of how they would affect operations, expressed general satisfaction with keeping things how they were.

Subsequent interactions with this doctor made it clear that he wasn't anti-growth or obstructionist. And, the marketing director wasn't haphazard or careless. But because neither paused to consider the engagement state of the other significant friction had formed.

Isolating this one exchange and re-engineering it shows the potency of mindset and congruence. The doctor was in a complacent state. He was tired and had just recently felt he'd gained a handle on how to effectively see the current flow of patients. The marketing director was in a invested state. Rather than seeing others for where they were and congruently tailoring to prompt an elevating effect, they interacted with each from their own present state.

What emerged was similar to someone who speaks Spanish and someone who speaks French increasingly speaking louder to the other, in his or her own language, and then storming off when the desired response isn't received. What was needed was congruent appreciation for the other's current state and then strategic elevation.

Until that point, they'd only negatively frustrated the shaping process.

The power of congruence is the ability to dynamically self-direct; to genuinely 'get it' across a variety of settings and circumstances. It is to accurately identify one's current state and to know how to positively affect it. And, to do the same with others.

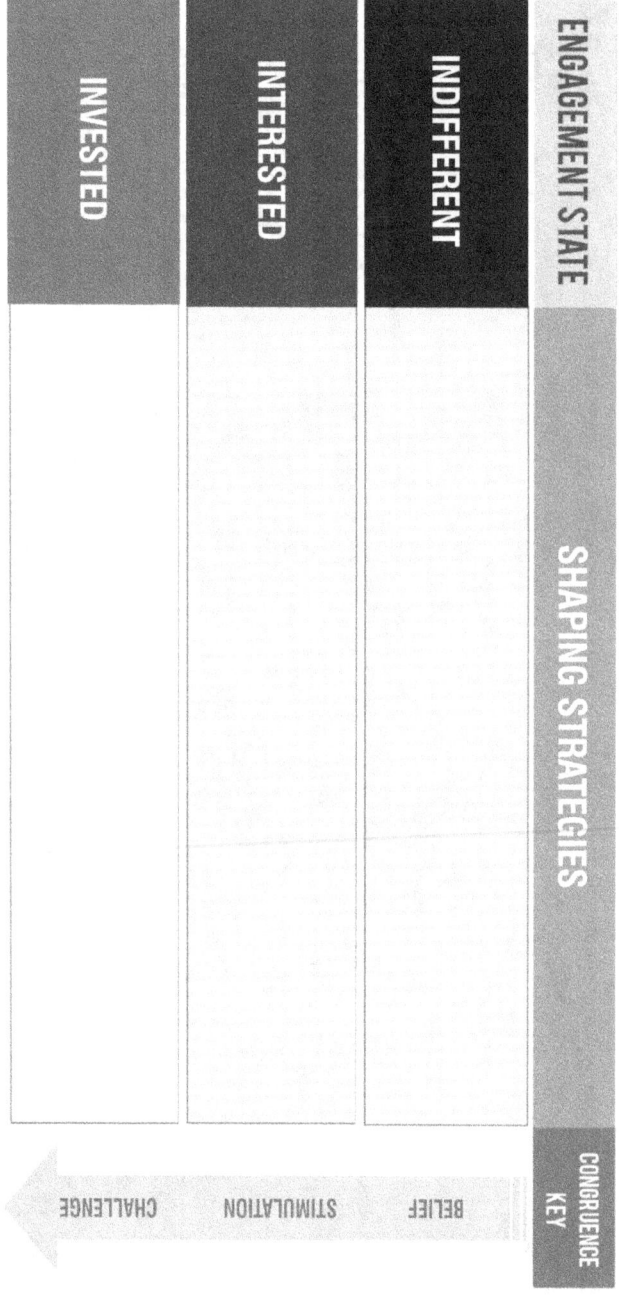

Figure 14

ENGAGEMENT GRID

ENGAGEMENT STATE	KEY ACTIVITY PERCEPTION	THOUGHT INDICATORS	DESCRIPTION OF RESULTS	LIKELY OUTCOME
INDIFFERENT	Important **NO** Meaningful **NO**	"This isn't for me." "I can't keep this up." "It doesn't matter." "Someone else can do this." "They don't get it/me."	Very little real work gets done Activities are overwhelming Takes circumstance view High energy for low results	Below Expectations
INTERESTED	Important **YES** Meaningful **NO**	"Think of the possibilities." "If I do this now it will payoff in the future." "This will be worth it." "Why not me?"	Deadlines and goals drive greater results Looks for greater capacity /self and others Efficient; results equal to energy exerted	Exceeds Expectations
INVESTED	Important **YES** Meaningful **YES**	"I love what I do." "I'm very grateful." "I want to share what has helped me." "How can this be more valuable?" "Let's make this a reality."	Attracts input, ideas, and referrals without asking Engages others well and often Consistently seeks out valuable advantages Results outweigh energy exerted	Outstanding

Figure 15

DISCOVERY SECTION

PART I: RESPOND

Respond to the questions below using the following rating scale:

A = Always. B = Often. C = Sometimes. D = Rarely. E = Never.

22. How often do you address indifference with its primary need?

23. How often do you address being interested with its primary need?

24. How often do you advance from interested to invested?

PART II: DESCRIBE

For the following prompt, describe how you would most likely respond. To get the most from your efforts, **don't** describe what you *think you should do*, but rather *what you would most likely do* based on how you've responded to similar situations in the past.

You want to have an impact and sense that it's important to do some things differently.

DISCOVERY SECTION

Consider the statement "The power of congruence is the ability to dynamically self-direct; to genuinely 'get it' across a variety of settings and circumstances. It is to accurately identify one's current state and to know how to positively affect it. And to do the same with others" and outline what in your current approach reinforces this and what could change to better harness congruence.

DISCOVERY SECTION

PRACTICE ACTIVITIES SECTION

Compare two scenarios from your recent experiences involving congruence — one more and one less successful. What did you think about prior to the outcome? How prevalent was your sense of gratitude? How did your mindset possibly influence the result?

- Experience #1 — More Successful

- Experience #2 — Less Successful

DISCOVERY SECTION

Given a similar scenario going forward, how could you build from the more successful elements and improve on the less successful ones?

CHAPTER 9

REINFORCE YOUR **AGENCY**

Conditions were the ideal blend of blue skies, fresh powder, and crisp winter air. The pair heading towards the slope shared a lot in common — except snowboarding. One had spent considerable time in the mountains and looked forward to a great day on the snow. The other was attempting the sport for the first time.

> "Shift your weight slightly to the front foot and steer with your back foot."

Because of their experience difference they'd agreed to split up and then meet back together for dinner. The more experienced snowboarder passed along some technical pointers and headed to the more challenging runs.

The less experienced friend was certain others could see him internally repeat the words shared with him as he got ready to catch his own chairlift.

> *Weight slightly forward.*
> *Steer with the back.*
> *Weight slightly forward.*
> *Steer with the back.*

By the time the beginning snowboarder reached the top of his slope he'd mentally rehearsed the words so many times a sense of confidence took over. Looking down the mountain he mentally reviewed the instructions one more time and pointed his snowboard down the hill.

The words didn't take.

He made it a few meters, caught a sharp edge as his snowboard dug into the snow, and crashed violently. It wasn't the kind of crash that leads to injury, but like accidently touching a low voltage wire it sent a sharp jolt through his body.

> *I didn't follow the instructions right.*
> *Weight slightly forward.*
> *Steer with the back.*

Convinced he'd simply miss-acted the guidance he was given he awkwardly made his way to his feet and again faced his board downhill.

Crash.

The impact of the first fall was somewhat masked by the adrenaline of trying to make his way down a 12,000-foot snowcapped mountain on what felt like an oversized skateboard without wheels. He felt every bit of the second fall.

The next several hours into the afternoon were spent repeating a similar, painful process. Point downhill, press his weight slightly forward, prepare to steer with his back foot (this part was almost never needed as he would fall after a few meters), and crash.

Convinced he'd found the most worthless sport on the planet as he lay in the snow from his latest fall, other snowboarders rushing by him on either side, he'd had enough. He was done playing the role of a puppy trying to run across a sheet of ice. He would carry his board and slide his way down the mountain to the lodge below. This miserable day would be over and he could start to heal the aches and bruises he'd accumulated from his falls.

"I don't think you want to go down that way"

He'd only been at it a minute or two, but that was long enough to want to crawl into a corner and erase the day from memory — especially now that he realized others noticed him haplessly making his way down the mountain on his backside. He must have looked ridiculous, he thought, as he sheepishly looked up to meet the eyes of a voice he didn't recognize.

"I'm terrible at this."

Of all the things he could have said he's not sure why those were the words that came out. The stranger mercifully leaned closer to give the appearance that they were just two acquaintances talking mid-slope and continued to listen.

"I did just what my friend told me, but it's not working."

"What did he tell you to do?"

He'd repeated the words so frequently they could nearly speak for themselves.

"Shift your weight slightly forward and steer with your back foot."

"No offense to your friend, but forget that."

His words were initially met with skepticism as the mood wasn't exactly primed for more 'magical advice.'

The stranger continued.

"I see this all the time. People get handed these steps to follow and they don't work."

In a sea of passersby, the guy was kind enough to stop so he'd earned a level of attention. Sensing the opening he kept going.

"Forget about your feet. Just relax and point your head in the direction you want to go. Wherever your head points your shoulders and the rest of you will follow."

The stranger helped the snowboarder up and said it one more time before heading down the mountain himself.

"Seriously. Stop thinking about your feet. Just stand up and focus on your head. Wherever it points the rest of your body will loosen and follow."

My friend was that snowboarder. And the very next run was the first time all day he made it down the mountain. Then he did it again. And again.

Forget about your feet. Focus on your head and the rest of you will follow.

MENTAL CONTRACTS

The inclination when trying to improve performance is to turn to one's feet. Seek out and follow a simplistic five step approach, copy the movements of another, or to just work the plan harder are common techniques when wanting to improve outcomes. And they fundamentally misunderstand what needs to happen first.

It's not the steps that provide the spark, but the idea to have an idea. Ordering matters. Think of the difference between relying on a cheat sheet of math proofs to do well on a test — and then realizing the questions were changed at the last minute — rather than genuinely understanding the concepts that will be tested. If the focus is placed entirely on the list of steps, or routines, or habits they will eventually fail when presented with a challenge that seems too great, they don't take on personal meaning, or the context shifts and one doesn't know how to adapt. Only the mindset can self-rejuvenate and take a learning orientation; to have the idea to have an idea. Then to wisely refine it. And do it again if necessary.

Focus on your head and the rest of you will follow.

The late Andy Grove, Intel's first employee and among its most influential CEO's, understood how this works as he consistently reimagined the technology space and Intel's advantaged role in it. While the company had produced interesting products prior to Grove's tenure, it was under his watch that *Intel inside* became not only a widely recognized slogan by the general public but deeply revered in the strategy field.

Grove was an unlikely candidate for such lofty achievements. Born in Budapest, Hungary he lived there until age eight when the Nazis invaded the country. Of Jewish decent, his family assumed false identities and moved around the country to avoid the concentration camps. He later escaped the political upheaval of the 1960's Hungarian revolution by moving to Austria and later to the United States. Once in the U.S. he went to university in New York and then earned a doctorate from UC-

Berkeley. It was from Berkeley that he first hired on with Intel.[122] [123] [124] [125] [126] [127]

According to firm documents it was under Grove's leadership that Intel transformed from a memory chip company to the world's largest manufacturer of semiconductors and helped to usher in the PC era. Revenues during that time grew from $1.9 billion to over $26 billion.

While much of this growth is attributed to the firm's radical strategy refinement, the development and execution of that plan were equivalent to the firm's feet. More interesting is to appreciate where the head pointed before the body ever moved.

For many $1.9 billion in revenues and an envied position as pioneer in the technology industry is an incredible deed — one worth simply maintaining. Grove imagined the potential for much deeper advantages. He asked, *what if intel processors were the power behind the vast majority of the world's computing technology?*

To tackle that question meant the firm would have to write a new mental contract. No longer would they simply be a memory chip company, but rather an intensively focused semiconductor manufacturer with a compelling proposition to make *intel inside* a cornerstone in the technology industry's rapid development. Grove worked tirelessly to point the firm's head in that direction (first his own, then others') — and the feet followed.

---

122 Grove, Andrew S. Swimming Across: a Memoir, Hachette Book Group (2001) Prologue
123 Isaacson, Walter (1997-12-29). "TIME: Man Of The Year" Time.
124 "Former Intel chief Andrew Grove dies aged 79", BBC, March 22, 2016
125 "Andy Grove, Valley Veteran Who Founded Intel, Dies at 79", Bloomberg, March 21, 2016
126 Gaither, Chris (2001-11-12). "Andy Grove's Tale of His Boyhood in Wartime". The New York Times. Retrieved September 04, 2016.
127 https://newsroom.intel.com/news-releases/andrew-s-grove-1936-2016/. Retrieved September 4, 2016.

When Kevin Lobo assumed the CEO position at billion-dollar medical devices firm, Stryker, a similar mental shift occurred. Previously an individual product centered firm, Lobo quickly identified the complacency in pumping out products that didn't begin from the patient and customer view. He explained that the firm needed to take on a new mindset that asked, "If you add this who's going to pay for it? That wasn't a thought (before)."[128] This new mental approach opened the firm to not only more valuable innovation opportunities, but new emerging markets. Over the next four years the company made ten key acquisitions, radically transformed its innovation strategy to a more collaborative model, and added hundreds of millions of dollars in revenues from previously underserved markets. Most operating and profitability metrics also improved during that time.[129] [130]

The examples continue. The post-Steve Ballmer Microsoft era began with tremendous uncertainty. He'd been with co-founder John Gates from the company's early stages and served as CEO from 2000-2014. At the time of his departure the firm was at crossroads. They had revolutionized the PC industry and were wildly profitable, but many wondered if they were flat lining as other technology firms such as Google seemed to be the hotter commodity.

To compound matters, the person succeeding Ballmer was not widely known. An internal hire, Satya Nadella was respected by his peers but had never previously been a CEO. Conditions were ripe for him to fall prey to one of two new leader traps. Both place the feet before the head. The first is to quickly launch multiple initiatives to stamp one's name on things (strategic confusion often results). The second trap is to assert one's voice so strongly, outwardly demonstrating how much one knows, that others don't find space for their own. Both share roots in a simple

---

128 http://www.fiercebiotech.com/medical-devices/stryker-ceo-touts-paradigm- shift Retrieved October 1, 2016.
129 http://phx.corporate-ir.net/phoenix.zhtml?c=118965&p=irol- newsArticle&ID=2139404. Retrieved September 3, 2016
130 http://careers.stryker.com/assets/en-us/pdfs/SYK-factsheet-April-2015.pdf Retrieved October 12, 2016.

axiom — if you're too consumed with the title of a position (its feet) you'll likely struggle to effectively tap its potential.

Nadella's results in the first two years of assuming the position suggest he didn't fall prey to either trap (one indicator, price per share, grew roughly 50% during that time). He paused and he listened. He considered the current state of the firm's culture and what it would need to be in order to drive the breadth and style of innovation the firm required. Soon powerful ways to reimagine the company and its offerings bubbled up. The firm's role as vibrant ecosystem keystone took new shape, one that welcomed interaction and strategic collaboration, and replaced divisive and resource-draining struggles with competitors. His investment in a new mental contract for himself and the firm — a learning orientation that sunk in deeply as he considered the role of the head before the feet and encouraged others to do the same — had taken root.

In his words, "I need to be able to walk out of here this evening and say, *where was I too closed-minded, or where did I not show the right kind of attitude of growth in my own mind?*"[131]

In each of these cases it's as if those involved had channeled the words of Ralph Waldo Emerson,

"Give me *truths*; for I am weary of the surfaces."[132]

The legal world provides a useful analogy. Contracts are agreements intended to be enforceable. They are expected to provide the *truths* to how things should function. Some do just that and provide tremendous operating clarity in a wide range of circumstances and across time. But not all contracts are equal. Some are poorly or lopsidedly devised, others unclearly written, and nearly all grow obsolete if not updated from time to time. Worse, these same contracts are considered binding despite missing the mark. When we enter into bad agreements, we're bound to fulfill terms that should have never existed.

---

131 http://www.bloomberg.com/features/2016-satya-nadella-interview-issue/ Retrieved September 6, 2016.

132 Emerson, W. (1929) Blight. The Complete Writings of Ralph Waldo Emerson, New York: Wm. H Wise & Co. 874.

One of transcendent music artist Little Richard's early record deals was this type of agreement. At one point Art Rupe, owner of Specialty records purchased the rights to the globally famous hit song "Tutti Frutti" for a reported $50 USD. Viewed from Little Richard's perspective this was a terrible deal. The artist was left receiving half a cent royalty per record at the valued rate — into perpetuity.[133]

Everyone has a mental contract — an internal agreement governing one's outlook at different points in time. Depending on how well it was originally crafted it may be partially or altogether obsolete. At minimum, it may have small cracks that will turn to chasms if untended. Yet, like a legal contract, despite being flawed or outdated these mental agreements will continue to be dutifully followed until an alternative approach takes root.

Regardless of your starting place, the invitation is to re-write that mental contract by more deeply considering the role mindset plays in outcomes. A single question can provide the initial spark,

> *Should we be doing it this way just because it's always been done this way?*

In some areas the answer will be 'yes.' Asking the question provides validation. In other ways honestly asking the question will highlight ways to more fully appreciate the Shaper cycle, better detect layers of engagement in yourself and others, and congruently approach these states to tap the best parts in each — ultimately driving towards the invested. As previously unseen opportunities materialize, confidence grows and the techniques reinforce. What might have previously felt strained becomes natural.

---

133 White, C. (2003) The Life and Times of Little Richard, United Kingdom: Omnibus Press; 3rd edition.

DATES AND DASHES

A frigid morning at the base of the Rocky Mountains found a man in his mid-thirties pulling onto the gravel drive of a small-town cemetery. He was in the area for business and took the occasion to visit the grave sites of his deceased grandparents. Stepping from the car he breathed in deeply and looked over the placid scene of fresh white snow covering the small plot of land.

He might have paused from the abrupt greeting of the winter air, but there was something more intentional to the way he stopped and surveyed the setting. This was sacred ground to him and he was giving it respect.

Much of what he now considered valuable as a man he learned as a boy on the acreage abutting that cemetery. The back portion of his grandparents' land formed its western property line and was easily visible from where he had parked. He stood there for several minutes — still as a palace guard. Perhaps the man had become a boy again as memories on that small farm washed over him.

When he emerged from that moment there was nothing abrupt to his movements. He simply turned and started walking towards the grave markers.

His pace was at first methodical. But after a few minutes of walking back and forth through several different rows it started to quicken. This might have gone unnoticed, but for his next move which looked like a near-frantic search as he speed-walked between the cemetery's roes–searching.

Then he found it.

Looking over the upright headstone he dropped to his knees and slowly reached forward. The snow had distorted his view for a time, but now he was at the place he intended. The granite was cold to the touch as he gently stroked its etchings, but he hardly seemed to notice. Sharing a burial site and headstone the way they'd shared so many other things in life — graciously — the markings depicted each of their names, their birth and death dates, and a sentence at the bottom that began with the word,

"Devoted."

The man later described in a series of conversations what had taken place.

> "Not finding them immediately really hit me. They hadn't moved. I had. That experience brought things into focus. When most people go to a cemetery, the first thing they do is look at the dates. If they give it a second thought they'll mentally calculate how long someone lived. To me it's not about the dates. It's about the space in between those two numbers. It's about that space being as rich and vivid and purposeful as possible. I see an elderly man manually siphoning gas from his old pick-up truck when he thought I wasn't looking and transferring it to my car as a college student so I'd have extra gas that week. I see an older woman, stately in character more than possessions, patiently walking the garden's rows holding a young boy's hand and helping him to pick out the vegetables they'd use for dinner that evening. I see through a slightly cracked bedroom door in mid-day the silhouette of a magnificent couple in their eighties, six decades into life together, stealing a silent dance before getting back to the work of serving the children and grandchildren who'd come to visit. I see strength. And grace. And conviction. I see people who weren't distracted by what didn't matter and who were never too busy to do the things that did. I see lives — fully lived."

When hearing this story, few argue that they don't crave something similar for themselves. Not the relationship alone (though incredibly admirable), but the sense of deep commitment it conveys and the legacy it symbolizes. They want the dash to be their focal point — not the dates. In the sensation of the moment some even ask about specific activities the couple did and then jot them down as to-do list notes soon forgotten.

But others see it as intended — to provide a trigger and then space to personalize the concept in meaningful ways. To focus on the head and anchor their impressions deeply so the rest of the body can follow in dynamic, lasting ways across a variety of circumstances. To re-write their mental contract.

Combining two different observations of classical essayist Oscar Wilde,

> "Discontent is the first step in the progress of a man. To live is the rarest thing in the world. Most people exist, that is all."[134] [135]

Discontent in the positive form isn't a call to clam up or to project or to retreat but an awakening to the capacity for improvement. It is the view that regardless of starting point, circumstances (and one's interactions with them) can be shaped to something better. And mindset is the necessary gateway. It allows for dynamic updating (consistently relevant mental contracts) and tapping 'needs' congruence. It achieves what other strategies do not. Whether CEO of a multi-billion-dollar firm, athlete, grandparent hoping to leave a mark or anyone in between the promptings sound similar and the process to unlock them is the same.

SHIFT

Thomas Kuhn first popularized the phrase 'paradigm shift' when he described that breakthrough science doesn't progress in a strictly linear way. Instead, it undergoes periodic, transformative upheavals.[136] These disruptions contribute to and benefit from new inquiry in ways clinging to prior knowledge, alone, could not.

Here the term 'shift' is informed by Kuhn's early work and describes a willing, positive break from one's status quo understanding because of new, compelling evidence and experience. More specifically, appreciating the Shaper cycle and its related parts can lead to significant breakthroughs in just about any conceivable productivity metric. But there's a catch.

Shifts don't happen without opposition. Current perceptions and understandings can be used to shrug off something new. Creative thinking can be judged by conventional biases. Imagine dismissing

---

134 Wilde, O. (1908). A Woman of No Importance: A Play. London: Methuen.
135 Wilde, O. (1914). The Soul of Man. Humphreys.
136 Kuhn, T. S. (2012). The structure of scientific revolutions. University of Chicago press.

early-staged computers because they weren't faster typewriters. Through history's lens this seems silly, but at the point of adoption the future trajectory wasn't so clear.

Anticipating resistance is key to writing a new mental contract. You don't have to know everything that will result. You just have to appreciate that mindset directly relates to results. And then start where you are.

While some will change their mindset because of a random positive event, more will assign that event to luck and not know how to repeat it. It's far more valuable to consider that breakthroughs tend to happen because of a changed mindset — not the other way around.

Once this is accepted a completely new way of thinking, discerning, and acting starts to form. Things aren't seen or experienced the same way ever again. What was previously overlooked is noticed. What were once voids become new opportunities. The invested mindset is desired, cultivated, and challenged. Dips into the indifferent or interested states are quickly recognized and course corrected. Each state can be identified and approached congruent to its primary needs (individually and interpersonally) — and elevated forward.

Focus on your head and the rest of you will follow.

The launch point is to realize: In every circumstance – there is choice.

DISCOVERY SECTION

PART I: RESPOND

Respond to the questions below using the following rating scale:

A = Always. B = Often. C = Sometimes. D = Rarely. E = Never.

25. How often do you keep with a given approach primarily because it has long been done that way?

26. How often does this statement describe you, "Some will change their mindset because of a random positive event, but more will assign that event to luck and not know how to repeat it"?

27. How often do you push through resistance when you know the effort is important and meaningful?

PART II: DESCRIBE

For the following question, describe how you would most likely respond. To get the most from your efforts, don't describe what you think you should do, but rather what you would most likely do based on how you've responded to similar situations in the past.

You know you need to change some actions. This has been difficult for you as you typically experience resistance when trying to do so. How would you likely respond in this situation?

DISCOVERY SECTION

Consider the statement, "Shifts don't happen without opposition. Never know too much to learn something new" and describe whether and how this relates to your current approach.

DISCOVERY SECTION

PRACTICE ACTIVITIES SECTION

Compare two scenarios from your recent experiences in which you attempted to re-write your mental contract — one more and one less successful. What explains the difference?

- Experience #1 — More Successful

DISCOVERY SECTION

- Experience #1 — More Successful (*continued*)

- Experience #2 — Less Successful

DISCOVERY SECTION

- Experience #2 — Less Successful (*continued*)

CHAPTER 10

PROVIDE **EFFECTIVE** FEEDBACK

"What I think we tend to not do well is to talk candidly."[137]
John Watson, former CEO, Chevron Corporation

---

137 Blogdet, H. The Business Insider Interview with John Watson. 21 May 2015.

Helping others to maximize their mental performance requires effectively giving and receiving vital feedback. While personality types and cultural influences range widely across individuals, each person's approach to candor falls into one of three categories: the ideal, the clam, or the projectile. The ideal, defined as the ability to communicate frankly *and* get a positive response even when conveying hard things, is the feedback goal. When this standard isn't met, either the clam or the projectile are usually found.[138]

THE CLAM

The clam approach is the avoidance of candor. It occurs when we know we should say something, but we swallow our words instead of expressing them or say what we think others want to hear rather than what they need to hear. Left unattended, this approach can cause us to withhold even the thoughts we think are most valid. The result is important things often go unexpressed, leaving holes in our interactions with others that lead to misunderstanding, mutual frustration, and the filling of gaps with assumptions.

For Susan, taking the clam approach when confronted with uncomfortable feedback situations had become her norm. Those close to her describe her as thoughtful and sweet, perhaps a little reserved; she cares about others' feelings, including how they feel about her, and generally prefers to keep the peace rather than to rock the boat. In her desire to protect others' feelings she often found herself swallowing her own. To her thinking, it was better to preserve her positive image than to express something that others might challenge. Some phrases she would mentally use to justify her approach included, "it's not really my business," "it's probably better for them to figure it out on their own,"

---

138 Some people are socialized through culture or other experiences to be more or less inclined to candor. This should be accounted for in yourself and others. Nonetheless, each of us must understand how to say and hear what is needed, how and when it's needed, in contextually relevant ways if we're to thrive in diverse settings. Based on working with people from nearly 30 countries and considering related research findings, this capability can be developed – regardless of your starting point.

"even if I say something it probably won't change anything," "maybe they know something I don't," "they should know better," and, "I don't want to get in the middle of it."

Susan realized the challenge to this approach when a couple close to her was having significant marital problems. It was clear to Susan that they were caught in a trap of self-deception, alternately blaming the other for issues they hadn't resolved themselves. Yet, in her desire to keep the peace she kept quiet. As the wife confided in Susan, Susan would listen and then simply agree with her or tell the wife what Susan thought she wanted to hear in the moment. After a few more months the marriage had deteriorated to the point that the couple hardly spoke to each other – they'd become indifferent to their marriage and their respective roles in it. Susan began to feel like she really needed to say something to them about her observations, but she just couldn't bring herself to do it – consistently telling herself it was none of her business. With each swallowed opportunity, however, Susan started to form her own guilt and eventually began to distance herself from people she previously cared for deeply.

There is plenty of empathy to go around for each participant in the above example, but let's focus on Susan because while she can't be expected to fix other people's problems she knew she should say something and didn't – which had the dual consequence of not improving the situation and creating her own mental headwind. Initially, Susan thought she was maintaining the peace and being gracious. But this is one of the great deceptions to clamming up: it is not generous to decline to share with someone what they may really need to hear. It is the opposite.

Why would people who on the surface seem to be agreeable choose an approach that leaves others fending for themselves, often at times when help is really needed?

The person who is likely to clam up thinks it is personally safer to appease others. Clamming up is a way to save our own interests from the commitment of expressing well what we really see and think. In personal interactions, the interests someone who clams up will often try to save relate to emotional preservation (e.g. wanting to avoid the stress of saying something contrary to what someone may want to hear, the need to appear pleasing to others, or the commitment it will take to work through potential disagreement). In professional settings with authority structures, the fear of retribution from someone with power to influence our prospects and the hope for political gain by appeasing others rather than dealing directly with them can prompt people to withhold candor. Despite the competing influences noted above, a common theme people describe in both personal and professional settings is, "Honestly, I wish I had the courage to raise my voice much more often and the skill to do it well."

It's a misnomer that saying nothing has no consequence. Inaction rarely leads to positive outcomes. In reality, saying nothing can often be as detrimental as saying the wrong thing. It is like a responsible adult seeing a child wandering in the street and doing nothing to intervene. Left unaddressed, the clam approach can promote an underlying detachment in difficult situations, needless amounts of ambiguity in their interactions, and the internal tension that comes from knowing one thing and doing another.

Clamming up also leaves those around you wondering if you are withholding information, which damages trust. It is human nature to fill these gaps. Without your messages to serve this role, others will invent stories to take their place.

The clam effect has major implications for organizations. Whenever ambiguity is present the potential for error increases.[139] This potential is compounded when ambiguity shifts from semantic misunderstanding (misdiagnosing the meaning of the words) to the lack of communication altogether. Catastrophic failures as grave as airliner fatalities (for example, Korean Air's safety record during the 1980's and 1990's[140])

---

[139] Gorfein, D. S. (Ed.). (2012). *Resolving semantic ambiguity.* Springer Science & Business Media.

[140] "Fatal Events Since 1970 for Korean Air", http://www.airsafe.com/events/airlines/kal.htm. Taken 20 July 2014.

have been linked, in part, to the inability or unwillingness of operators to communicate candidly with support crew. Though some forms of ambiguity are rooted in centuries of high context cultural norms (contextual elements – e.g. tone, status, body language – primarily govern the rules of communication and not explicit statements), these norms can be re-imagined when the need arises. An important factor to Korean Air's safety turnaround was to systematically push through the clam effect to create training and communication norms that greatly reduced ambiguity and increased trust – all while using pilots from the same cultural upbringing that had experienced the abysmal safety record just years earlier.[141]

For every major event there are many smaller events with their own compounding effect on performance potential. An extensive Gallup study of 25,000 managers and executives highlights what can happen when people feel disconnected from their peers and organizations.[142] 71% self-identified as not engaged or actively disengaged from their work. A frequent cause of disengagement is the belief that one's interests and voice are not heard – the sense that it is unsafe or not worth it to openly share feedback and ideas. This belief impacts emotional engagement, resulting in unnecessary silence and marginal (or, at minimum, diminished) effort. Gallup estimates that this effect costs organizations a staggering $450 to $550 billion dollars per year in lost productivity.

THE PROJECTILE

The other end of the spectrum is the projectile approach - the misuse of candor. This is when we say what we think without regard for our

---

141 Geoffrey, T. The yin and yang of Korean Air: the airline appears to have achieved an operational and safety rebirth that is paving the way for a new era of growth and profitability." (Statistical Data Included) Air Transport World. 1 Oct. 2015.

142 Gallup study http://www.gallup.com/poll/150383/majority-american-workers-not-engaged-jobs.aspx. Taken 1 Oct. 2015. http://www.gallup.com/businessjournal/162953/tackle-employees-stagnating-engagement.aspx. Taken 1 Oct. 2015.

approach. Just as clamming up is fool's gold, it is not courageous to arbitrarily dump our opinions on others for them to resolve. Ultimately, for effective candor to take form we must realize that we can't expect others to simply deal with our words. It's an error to think that it doesn't matter how we express ourselves if we are able to get things off our chest. How we say things directly influences another's willingness to listen.

Why would otherwise intelligent people misuse candor in this way?

The projectile approach is frequently present in both professional and personal settings, and can be used with those we know both well and in passing. In other words, this approach does not discriminate as much by setting as it does by your mindset in the moment and your perceived role in the relationship. Recognizing that this approach is often prompted by a sense of entitlement (the belief that you deserve something), power (ability to affect others' outcomes), or self-justification (excusing your own role in a situation) can help you to understand what it may mean when you use it or when others use it with you.

Recognizing underlying motives in the projectile approach can help explain why its use is not likely to lead to mutually beneficial exchanges. When projecting, we tend to be blinded by interests outside our own – looking past the person being addressed. This mindset is indicative of someone who tends to believe that getting the words out is sufficient and it is up to the listener to make sense of them – the message giver's only role is to convey whatever message s/he feels is important. Paradoxically, it is often an unresolved issue in ourselves that will prompt us to misuse candor in this way – we project onto others more than their share of the dissatisfaction, entitlement, or stress we may feel within ourselves.

Thoughts that are prevalent when in projective feedback include, "it's not my job to figure it out for them," "I'm tired of pulling more than my weight," "I know what's best," "I don't care what others think," "I can't believe they did that," "He should know better," and "she needs to just listen." Perhaps more damaging, the projectile effect can be preceded by little thought at all – indicating we haven't considered our words before projecting them.

One sign you are in a projectile pattern is if you tend to quickly react to situations without fully considering the impact of your words and/or if you find your exchanges of disagreement with others frequently tipping into arguments or feuds (either heated or angry or passive-aggressive exchanges).

This misuse of candor can have damaging effects on social relationships and cripple the transfer of otherwise important messages. When misused, the two most common results are offense (perceiving what is said to be an insult) and defensiveness (protecting oneself from perceived threats). Offense is a powerful emotion that has ruined many previously healthy interactions. While we cannot always control whether or not another will take offense, our approach to feedback can greatly influence whether or not offense will result. Subsequent chapters consider how to give and receive feedback while minimizing the potential for offense.

To projectile can also prompt those around us to dismiss otherwise valid points because they're presented in a way that prompts defensive tendencies. Different from offense, defensiveness prods listeners to filter through messages and select only the parts they want to accept – like selectively plugging one's ears. Otherwise valid messages tend to go unheeded because of how they were presented. Witnessing the lack of action from the message's recipient can then prompt the sender to projectile more – determined to *really* make his or her point – which tends to deepen the defensiveness reflex in the recipient.

Projectiling forms a perverse relationship with interpersonal misunderstanding. The more we projectile, the less others want to listen. The less people show interest in listening, the more we'll want to projectile. Without an alternative strategy, it is unlikely our interactions with others will reach their potential.

Beyond personal interactions, the effects of projectiling and clamming up can often be found across power structures in organizations. A person in a position of authority is more likely to feel entitled to misuse candor because s/he doesn't have the same fear of retribution that a subordinate might feel. Recognizing this unpacks a serious dilemma that groups must confront; those in authority are often most detached from everyday reality (where great insights tend to reside) yet are more likely to projectile and talk over subordinates, while those who report to them are closer to market realities yet are more likely to clam up – creating a vacuum in the transference of vital information that could otherwise benefit the group. The best groups will recognize this and take measures to minimize its presence.

Perception is a powerful force that can skew our sense of reality. Understanding this is key to becoming comfortable with saying and hearing what matters most. Even before we interact with others, perception (what we *want* to see) can influence the way we view events. Distinguishing what we *ought* to see from what we *want* to see when giving and receiving feedback requires conscious effort; skewed perceptions can be subtle and defy what we would otherwise expect for a given scenario.

An experiment with drinking water shows how perception can influence actions. People from various walks of life are presented two options. One is an elegant looking, European-branded bottle filled with regular tap water. The other is an unmarked bottle filled with more expensive, higher quality mountain stream-purified water. Participants are asked to drink the water from each container and select which one tastes better.

The majority select the poorer quality water housed in the elegantly branded bottle. Why?

Their *perception* of quality (influenced by the bottles' packaging) overshadows the reality of what they're experiencing. They think the elegantly branded water *should* taste better, so they convince themselves that it does. We know this based on a second layer to the experiment. Without revealing the results from the first test, participants are presented a second chance to distinguish the water quality – but this time only unmarked bottles are used for both options. Presented this way, the majority accurately select the mountain stream-purified water.

In the first round, peoples' perception of what they think *should be* blinds them to the reality of *what really is* – a distinction they clearly identify in the second round. This example highlights important insights into the role perception can play in creating communication gaps between what we see and what others see.

The job of effective feedback is to help two or more people to mutually see and accept what really is – to minimize interpersonal gaps so that improvement can occur. To do this, it's important to recognize how personal interests can skew interpersonal exchanges and derail mutual understanding – making communications unnecessarily poor.

A straightforward way to think about this is to consider the difference between the motives to "be right" and to "get 'it' right." Trying to "be right" is the enemy to "getting 'it' right." The first is primarily concerned with validating preconceived opinions – often formed before an interaction even takes place. When trying to 'be right' your mind dismisses or bends otherwise valid information because this new information disagrees with your pre-conceived opinions. 'Get 'it' right' is concerned with mutual understanding and the reality of events, regardless of one's own opinion.

Recognizing these patterns is key. Self-awareness is a powerful behavioral tool that can highlight when our actions don't match our intentions (or when our intentions are off track) – when we need to shift from doing one thing to doing something else in order to get the desired result. It's important to become familiar with when you and others are trying to "be right" rather than trying to "get 'it' right."

Let's look at the two primary ways "be right" motives appear in day-to-day activities so we can recognize when they're influencing our interactions with others: 'Entrenchment' (clinging to our own position despite recognizing its flaws) and 'Fly-bys' (exchanging words without seeing the other's point of view).

ENTRENCHMENT

Several years before the passing of Fidel Castro, a management researcher experienced entrenchment first hand on assignment in Cuba to help develop relations for a talent development program. While in the country, he talked with several people or their descendants who had participated in the Castro-led revolution. As trust grew, they shared their thoughts with him. Years later the tone of a particular gentleman is still vivid - shared with the researcher as they sat in casual conversation in the open air of old Havana with the city's dynamic sounds humming in the background.

It was clear this man had his pulse on the thoughts and feelings of a generation (his father had participated with Castro in toppling the Batista regime). They were disappointed with the results of the revolution. But it was equally clear that they wanted to preserve their personal stake in it.

Presenting his father's words this man explained, "It didn't work out the way they planned. And clearly there is a lot wrong with the current system. But even knowing that it didn't work out well in the end, to go back and feel what they felt in the moments of the revolution, they'd do it all over again." These words were affirmed by others who participated in that movement through other conversations, sometimes joined with dogged defiance - as if their now aged bodies would be willing to risk the jungle marches again if asked.

How can people admit one thing yet cling to its opposite? This wasn't a matter of them being self-deceived or not understanding the situation. They recognized the failure of their activities and yet were willing to repeat them. Regardless of your political persuasion, this example highlights how powerful emotional entrenchment can be.

The danger with entrenchment is that it closes people off to alternative views before they're fully considered. When deeply embedded in someone, it is hard for that person to have candid dialogue with others about topics they disagree with or find risky or uncomfortable. So, in these scenarios he or she will seek information that affirms his or her positions and try to dismiss information that does not – reducing the window for discussing information outside that narrow view.

It may not take you long to think of someone in your life who primarily communicates from a position of "being right." What are your thoughts when you interact with that person? What is the quality of your interactions?

Because the world is so dynamic and no two people experience it exactly the same way it's critical that entrenchment be minimized. While present to some extent in all of us as we seek validation of our own positions and attempt to cover vulnerabilities, it doesn't have to be overpowering in any of us.

Entrenchment is often fear or insecurity falsely masquerading as self-assuredness. It's trading the beneficial kind of vulnerability that builds trust for pretense (an attempt to make something false appear true). Some of its symptoms are exaggeration, dismissiveness, and judgment. Seeing this pattern helps us to understand one of the ways we interact with others from a position of "being right" – almost assuring the quality of our interactions will be wrong.

Recognizing entrenchment in others is easier than admitting it in ourselves. To initially understand how prone to entrenchment you are and how it may influence your interactions with others, ask yourself a few questions (Table 3.1).

EXHIBIT

Questions to Consider

- When is the last time you admitted to another that you were wrong about something important to you and then changed your behavior?
- When was the last time you changed your opinion when presented with new evidence?
- When was the last time you avoided getting offended after being told something that was hard for you to hear?

The less entrenched you are the easier it should be to provide examples to these questions.

FLY-BYS

'Fly-bys' occur when two or more people experience the same event or conversation, but see it differently. While we all fundamentally share much in common, we also bring unique thoughts and social experiences to situations – raising the potential for fly-bys. You can probably think of at least one fly-by you've witnessed in the last day alone.

The exchange between two capable professionals, Samuel and Tina, shows how a fly-by can look. Both are intelligent, college-educated adults who work together in a volunteer organization in their community. During a conversation about an event they were planning together, which would include a physical activity to test participant's teamwork skills, Samuel expressed concern that adding more people to Tina's oversight group would be important to ensure everyone's safety. Samuel wouldn't be able to personally attend, and thought by suggesting others get involved he was being thoughtful and minimizing potential risk.

Tina heard something entirely different. Even though she enjoyed Samuel's help in these activities, she heard in his comments that he doesn't trust her to do them well in his absence – she's not capable without others' involvement. She took the position of describing to Samuel that he needn't worry – she had thought through things and had already considered what was needed. What she heard in Samuel's words wasn't confidence in her, but rather concern that things wouldn't go well unless Jim or those he suggested were present.

We talked with both individually after the exchange. It was clear that neither intended any malice. Samuel honestly thought he had Tina's and the activity's best interests at heart. Tina thought the same. Yet, each of them interpreted their conversation completely differently.

Neither Samuel nor Tina is right. Fly-bys aren't a matter of assigning blame; they're wrong because understanding isn't reached regardless of who's participating – but usually not because one party intends the other harm. Like an open space that needs to be filled, when fly-bys occur each participant's perception of the exchange simply takes over.

Left unattended, however, fly-bys will create cracks in any interaction, relationship, or team – which can then result in discomfort, ill-feelings, the guarding of information, or other negative outcomes.

An observation activity conducted with a large international organization to consider the number of fly-by incidents they experienced over a month highlights how pervasive these experiences can be. Both inward (employee to employee) and outward (employee to client or supplier) interactions were considered. Not saying what was needed (clamming) – triggering confusion, uncertainty, assumptions, or mistrust – and saying something poorly (projectiling) – prompting heightened emotions, disinterest, dismissiveness, or skepticism – were the primary fly-by symptoms considered.

The standard for fly-bys in this exercise was rigorous to ensure their occurrence was clear - a fundamental misunderstanding between two or more people requiring follow-up clarification had to take place to qualify as a fly-by. An above average performing team of 23 members was selected. Our purpose was not disclosed so we could observe people acting in natural ways.

In one month across a team of 23 individuals nearly 400 fly-bys were identified – an average of about 1 a day/per person. If a firm has just 500 employees who perform similarly to this group they will experience over 10,000 fly-bys *each month* – all of them representing the potential for wasted resources, interpersonal friction, misinformation, lost clients, and increased liability. In an educated organizational setting where people are at least mindful of the importance of communicating well, effective candor alluded them far more than necessary. It's not hard to envision the opportunity for development. The need isn't going to go away so our skills must get better.

EXHIBIT

Questions to Consider

- Do others often misunderstand your intentions?
- Do you often need to repeat yourself to others or receive responses from them that are different than you expected?
- Do you get frustrated when dealing with people who see things differently?

The less prone to 'fly-bys' you are the fewer examples will likely come to mind.

GET 'IT' RIGHT IS THE GOAL

Bridging perception gaps (getting to mutual understanding) requires actively trying to get 'it' right. 'It' is a shared interest that evokes joint ownership in what is right. This is the starting place to saying and hearing what matters most without giving or taking offense - even when dealing in risky or uncomfortable situations. A two-by-two box is a helpful way to consider the relationship between the desire to get 'it' right and competency of the communicator.

COMMUNICATOR SKILL (Perceived Competence)	Low MOTIVE TO GET 'IT' RIGHT (Perceived Intention)	High MOTIVE TO GET 'IT' RIGHT (Perceived Intention)
High	Well-articulated, but mistrusted message	Understood and trusted message (promoting a positive outcome)
Low	Mistrusted & misunderstood message	Trusted, but misunderstood message

Effectively giving feedback requires a combination of conveying the right motive (others perceive your interests or motives as benevolent; to improve rather than to impose) and expressing yourself clearly; combining will (interest and courage) and skill (effective techniques/ approaches).

In a long-running reality television show one of the main characters was famous for berating business owners - shocking them into listening to the advice that would follow. None of the businesses operated well, and many of the owners were in denial. The idea was to force people to admit the gravity of their situation – to make them confront reality. This approach can be characterized as 'break then build.'

Is this the most effective way to deal frankly with others? Candor is another way of expressing the need for change. Getting others to be real or to appreciate the magnitude of a situation is a critical first step. Social scientists have looked comparatively at the effectiveness between this and an alternate technique.

Breaking someone can seem natural to the survival instinct – inserting control or order into a situation. When the only objective is compliance (doing as you've been ordered) this approach can be effective – evidenced by military training or hierarchical organizational designs that lean on a command approach. Force, obligation, and fear are favorite tools in this approach.

The challenge with compliance, however, is it always requires a master – an external voice to give orders. Outside of life or death situations human tendency across varied cultures is to resent (and, eventually, resist) coercive masters. History is brightly colored with examples of rebellion against dominance and coercion; the desire for self-agency is fundamental to the human experience. Ironically, recipients aren't the only ones to become resentful in the compliance approach - the master him or herself can grow tired and resentful of constantly directing another's activities.

For any activity or social exchange to reach its full potential you must trust others will come through with their part when you're not looking.

Candor's best intention is to deepen connections and understanding among two or more people by dealing openly without fear of retribution. When compliance is the motive both the giver and the receiver are skeptical that the other will do their part without ongoing coercion. Fear and trust cannot mutually exist.

Cooperation (voluntarily doing what is desired) is very different from compliance. Though they share the same goal (effectively getting things done), cooperation appeals to peoples' desire to contribute rather than to their fear of non-compliance. Revisiting the television show example, participants are often shown to be taken back by the harshness with which they're treated (the 'break' part of compliance). Only once the 'build' approach begins does behavioral change take form. This is an appropriate metaphor for research into supportive vs. abrasive feedback. Shock-factor entertainment can translate poorly to actual interactions. As building is what ignites openness - that is where to begin.

More effective than breaking someone down only to build them back up is the approach 'build then bend.' This is no less direct (honest dealing is key), but its underlying techniques and goal of cooperation contrast sharply with simply compliance. Leading with a supportive (build) approach tackles defensive tendencies by encouraging people to consider the benefits of an alternate course rather than justifying failed behaviors.

HUMANS AND STEEL

Think of the process of forming steel. Heat in proper application is essential, but too much heat or heat exposure for too long will cause the steel to overly harden - and then to crack. Human interactions are similar. A level of candor (heat) is needed to bring clarity and, if necessary, gravity to an interaction. If your directness is overheated or overexposed, however, your efforts will backfire.

Appropriate heat is more supportive than dramatic. For example, "You can do this. This is what it will take" is more supportive (building) than "You're going to fail if you don't listen to me." "Things need to change. Let's talk about how to make that happen" is more supportive than "What's wrong with you?"

As steel is heated appropriately it becomes malleable – ready to bend. The same holds for people.

Heating (building) something for its own sake is pointless; you need to be ready with ideas about the form it should take – the path forward. Bending is most effective if both participants contribute to the process. The hero syndrome (seeking recognition by creating desperate situations for you to solve) will stunt the value of communications just as will telling someone they have a problem without contributing supportive thoughts for improvement.

You'll know when you've sufficiently built because the other's mannerisms and/or language will indicate openness to bending. This may include non-verbal tension cues relaxing, posture improving, eye contact enhancing, or affirmative statements being made, among others.

Providing high-impact feedback begins with recognizing a need and culminates with the willingness to do what that need requires. Plato outlined, 'the true creator is necessity, who is the mother of our invention'.[143] The challenge is many will misunderstand the process Plato described – believing the breakthrough should come simply because the need exists. It's hard to put in the effort before having a personal experience with the outcome, but you won't have a personal experience with the outcome until you put in the effort.

Every day you encounter opportunities to 'build then bend.' Whether in professional or personal settings, effectively providing feedback in ways that are congruent with the need can become your natural way of bringing out the Shaper benefits in others.

---

143 Plato's Republic, book II, 369C

DISCOVERY SECTION

PART I: RESPOND

Respond to the questions below using the following rating scale:

A = Always. B = Often. C = Sometimes. D = Rarely. E = Never.

Do you resist saying something if you think it will be unpopular?

When problems arise, do you initially avoid them?

DISCOVERY SECTION

Do you often say things without thinking them through?

Do others take offense or become defensive when you speak your mind?

How frequently do you get into arguments with others?

DISCOVERY SECTION

PART II: DESCRIBE

For the following questions describe how you would most likely respond. To get the most from your efforts, **don't** describe what you *think you should do*, but rather *what you would most likely actually do* based on how you've responded to similar situations in the past.

Someone you report to says something embarrassing about you in a group setting. Everyone laughed in good fun, but you didn't appreciate the comments. How would you likely respond in this the situation?

DISCOVERY SECTION

You are asked by someone close to you to give feedback about some work s/he has produced. You know s/he cares deeply about performing in this subject and s/he has expressed interest in doing more of this type of work. In reality s/he has limited talent in this area and you think s/he should pursue other things s/he would do better.

Would you likely try to preserve feelings or say what you actually think? Why?

PRACTICE ACTIVITIES SECTION

Over the next two days keep a record of the number of times your either clam up or projectile. What patterns do you see in the situations when you clam up (if applicable)? What patterns do you see in the situations when you projectile (if applicable)? Are you more likely to do one over the other? How would you describe the outcomes from using each of these approaches?

DISCOVERY SECTION

Select one of the times you clammed up and describe the personal interests you were trying to protect by avoiding candor with the other person. Try to see this event through your own motives and interests rather than through the other person. Then select a projectile event and describe the thoughts and feelings you had (if any) before speaking. Close by describing how the Congruence principle from Chapter 8 and effectively providing feedback work together.

CHAPTER 11

MAXIMIZING **MECHANISMS**

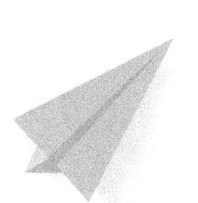

Shoot or don't shoot?

Tucked deeply into the Mojave Desert is a safety training facility that hosts thousands of clients annually. Among attendees are law enforcement personnel, military members, and civilians who want to use firearms responsibly. Lectures, scenario instruction, and simulations pace participants through mental and physical repetitions similar to actual situations. The danger of hesitating is a primary theme throughout.

One scenario is known informally as 'shoot or don't shoot.' Participants are grouped into a large classroom. The training focuses on building threat awareness and, when necessary, to understand proper defensive firearm use. To increase the intensity, instructors present scenarios placing people and things that participants love in harm's way.

Here's an example. You go to a bank late at night to withdraw money from the ATM. Confident in its use, you decided to take your firearm with you. The ATM is side-mounted against one of the banks exterior walls. Someone you love waits in the front passenger seat of the car while you get out to withdraw the money. While in the process of getting your money, you notice a figure standing in some trees just across the drive from you — less than

10 meters away. He's wearing a long coat and looks dangerous. His hands are suspiciously shoved into his pockets and appear to be clutching something, but you're not sure what it is.

You finish pulling the money from the ATM right as the man strategically traces a dimly-lit path towards you.

"Give me the money or I'm going to kill you."

The words instantly hit you. Almost like an out of body experience you have the sensation: *This isn't a simulation. This is real.*

You drop the money to the ground and tell the man he can have it as you slowly back away. As he goes to pick up the money you draw your handgun from its concealed position and point it at the man. You channel a commanding voice and tell him to take the money and leave.

He's not affected. Using one hand to fold the money from the ground into his coat — the other hand continues to be tucked into his pocket — he rises and stares directly at you.

"It's not enough. Withdraw everything you have or I'll kill you." At this point the instruction pauses.

"Shoot or don't shoot? How many of you wouldn't hesitate at that moment to kill this guy?"

Data from these scenarios show about one-third (1/3) of the room will initially stand up. More will then follow after seeing that there is safety in numbers — bringing the total to about one-half (1/2).

These groups tend to cluster into three camps. The first group is quick to stand. Their bias is towards usage and they're looking for sufficient prompts to do so. The second group wants to feel like they'd be willing to protect their loved ones, but doesn't show the same eagerness as the first group. They hesitate until the social temperature in the room gives them the confidence to stand. The final group struggles with the prospect of ending another person's life and elects to remain seated.

How would you respond to, "Shoot or don't shoot?"

Impulse can pull people strongly towards group one (shoot quickly) or group three (don't shoot at all) depending on embedded bias towards one or the other. When pressed the first group, otherwise law-abiding citizens, will error on the side of employing the skill they've obtained with a firearm. The third group will error on the side of preserving life — even to the danger of their own. Group two, or the hesitators, find themselves stuck in the middle and struggle to take a decision until social indicators become clearer (e.g. a large percentage of people stand up).

Observing these outcomes is fascinating. Even more interesting is what happens next.

"What about a third option to shoot or don't shoot?"

Instructors are typically met with confusion when they pose this question. Participants shuffle a bit and look around to test others' reactions. Some dig in deeper to one option or the other and try to convince those around them of the same.

Then more context is provided.

"The best answer is: why were you at a bank late at night withdrawing money in the first place? It's dark. The parking lot is nearly empty. There were probably half a dozen better times during the day you could have taken the ten minutes the task requires. Why put yourself or your loved one in that predicament? The situation could have been avoided completely with a bit more thought."

A single prompt promotes significant change.

The instruction closes with wording like the following,

> "The most valuable thing you can pull from this training is to become more mentally aware so you can make better choices; to avoid compromising scenarios altogether; to think about what success really looks like and put parameters in play to achieve it more often."

MECHANISMS

Mechanisms are means by which an effect is produced or a purpose is accomplished. Used well, they are the extra push turning intention to action. Structural elements that nudge behavior, they help to turn vision to output.

Mechanisms can be positive or negative depending on an idea's intent. Their job isn't to determine the quality of an idea; they just get the idea executed. The organizational world provides several examples of harmful and helpful mechanisms. We treat them in order starting with the negative (controls) and then moving to the positive (stimuli).

In every organization there are sources of influence outside of formal leadership. A temptation for leaders, therefore, is to consolidate that power. This often takes the form of control mechanisms such as increased reports and documents and bureaucratic measures that tend to corral behavior, but don't increase performance. These mechanisms don't give space for innovation and undermine the opportunity for exceptional results.

For example, one CEO we interviewed (for related work) personally tracks how many operations meetings his managers hold in a month and requires that they send him the total. The mechanism of having to report the total ensures that meetings are held, but it does little to influence their quality. The company's returns under that CEO consistently underperformed the broader industry.

Different than control mechanisms, stimulus mechanisms are intended to invigorate activity, to reduce wasted motion, and to better utilize resources. They achieve what controls cannot — structural support for the invested mindset.

Nordstrom's *'no questions asked'* return policy is one example. Every member of the organization knows that the customer has the power to vote on the quality of their service through this mechanism. Beyond this approach being positively perceived by customers, how many returns do you think it takes before a store gets very serious about unpacking the root cause of customer dissatisfaction?

Key to Nordstrom's vision is to be the leader in customer service. Rather than just say this they developed a structural stimulus that directly turns vision to action.

Consider how this could look in other organizations. What if a private preparatory high school offered a money back guarantee for those students who maintain a certain GPA (grade point average) but don't gain admission to one of their top ten university selections (which are identified their freshman year)? How many tuition refunds would the school absorb before seriously looking at its enrollment efforts, its placement efforts, and its relevance to current higher education demands? Not many. What message would this mechanism send to potential candidates in terms of how seriously the school views delivering an experience that aligns with the students' aspirations?

Mechanisms function similarly at the personal level. Things that are really worth pursuing require effort. Too often, however, effort is translated to mean herculean acts of will-power and self-determination available to few. Others will treat effort like a diet or fleeting trend, equally quick to ignite and to fizzle out. Goals are set with the best of intentions and then previous patterns re-emerge at the first sign of challenge or new fad.

Take sugar. Humans love it. But we also hate the effects of loving it and consistently look for ways to quit it. Rubber bands worn around the wrist to snap ourselves when tempted by it. Supplemental or alternative diets that repurpose or cut it out altogether — until it continues to knock at the door like a guest you can't decline. Creating clever laboratory versions of it meant to distract us from what we're actually consuming.

Part of the challenge is sugar serves a function. As Harvard evolutionary biologist Daniel Lieberman described,

"Since sugar is a basic form of energy in food, a sweet tooth was adaptive in ancient times, when food was limited. Simply put, humans evolved to crave sugar, store it and then use it."[144]

That equation was once in balance. Then came the extreme. Cheap sources of sugar were made available to bodies inclined to crave it. Once an indulgent, and rare, reward too frequently became a vicious cycle of craving, relenting, and loathing. Repeated.

To repurpose something as deep-seeded as sugar cravings, desire (in this case used synonymously with freewill) must be paired with mechanisms equal to the task. Otherwise, it's like placing someone in a store filled with their favorite sweet, indefinitely, and telling them not to succumb. There's a better way.

---

144 http://www.nytimes.com/2012/06/06/opinion/evolutions-sweet-tooth.html. Retrieved August 12, 2016.

Building on the sugar theme, the now famous Stanford Marshmallow Experiment received important updating when researchers at the University of Rochester primed participants to believe they were either in a reliable or an unreliable situation before performing the marshmallow task.

In the classic 1970's version children ages 4-6 (chosen, in part, because young children often struggle to delay gratification to achieve later, greater rewards — and some do this worse than others) were placed at a table one at a time with a tempting marshmallow staring at them. They were free to either eat the marshmallow right away or to wait fifteen (15) minutes and receive a reward: a second marshmallow. Most of the children gave in and ate the marshmallow within three minutes. The life outcomes of participants were tracked. Those who held out the entire 15 minutes went on to earn 210 points higher on the SAT than the children who didn't. They also enjoyed more success in relationships and better managed stress and attention as adults.[145] [146]

The original marshmallow test contributed key input to the value of patience, willpower, and delayed gratification, but it gives limited instruction for how to impact these areas. The Rochester version of the experiment provides further insight by adding a step before children have the option to eat the marshmallow.

Children were divided equally into two groups. Half of the kids were subjected to a broken promise regarding art supplies just before the marshmallow challenge. The other half were given the same promise about the art supplies, but this time the promise was completed. When it came time for the marshmallows, the rewarded children (those who'd experienced the kept promise) held out four times longer than their counterparts.[147]

---

145 Mischel, W., Ebbesen, E. B., & Raskoff Zeiss, A. (1972). Cognitive and attentional mechanisms in delay of gratification. Journal of personality and social psychology, 21(2), 204.

146 Mischel, W., Shoda, Y., & Rodriguez, M. L. (1989). Delay of gratification in children. Science, 244(4907), 933-938.

147 Kidd, C., Palmeri, H., & Aslin, R. N. (2013). Rational snacking: Young children's decision-making on the marshmallow task is moderated by beliefs about environmental reliability. Cognition, 126(1), 109-114.

The study suggests that children are much more willing to wait, on average twice as long, for the second marshmallow if they believe waiting will actually pay off. The mechanism of reliability, recently experiencing a broken or kept promise, significantly impacted the children's perception of value and their willingness to hold out for the larger reward. Their genetics didn't change in an instant. Nor did their level of intelligence. Everything else equal, one straightforward catalyst was decisive in turning interest to result.

Shaper is similar. Mental paths will follow existing patterns unless provided sufficient stimulus to embrace alternate routes. While the desire for change can happen at once, the work of change is more involved. Just how involved largely depends on the intensity of the desire and the quality of the mechanisms to support it.

Committing to effective shaping is a critical step. Its lasting effect, or ability to sink deeply and become the new norm, is aided by intelligently employing mechanisms that reinforce the value of greater rewards. Think of them as signs on a path reminding you to elevate your mindset; cues that being mentally alert sets into motion a process that produces better results and avoids simplistic alternatives (see the "shoot or don't shoot" example at the beginning of this chapter).

Mechanisms are at their best when those most impacted by them contribute to their design. Their purpose is straightforward; to provide follow-through support to an approach that's already been accepted or to an intention that needs to be reinforced.

Because effective Shaper isn't a philosophical quest to float around in a perpetual state of creativity, but rather a grounded approach to understand the relationship between mindset and outcomes, quickly identifying states of engagement and their fluid tendencies, skillfully unlocking their best parts (personally and interpersonally) towards the invested, and helping others to do the same its value is best found in its doing. The most refined mechanisms will encourage frequent, progressively effective use. Timing (immediacy), regularity (consistency), and efficacy (quality) matter. A viable campfire is not built all at once by throwing a match on massive logs and sitting around — hoping they'll burn. It happens by starting quickly (as soon as the idea to build a fire takes place) with small, dry kindling and an initial spark, nurturing the modest flame with oxygen, then adding increasingly larger wood to the mix in a patterned method until a vibrant, sustainable fire results. Because of the universal physics involved, as long as a viable source of fuel and the ability to spark it are present the process is repeatable.

Reliability is mutually reinforcing. The more often something valuable is done well the better the results. The better the results the more likely it will be repeated.

It is easy to short-change something if belief in its return is limited. The person hacking through the jungle with few provisions will only go so far before turning back.

This is particularly true if understanding of what's on the horizon is narrow — simply starring into a sea of trees. But what if partially climbing one of those trees reveals a small glimmer of water on the horizon? For how long and how intently will that person then carve through the jungle?

In the first option the water is never found nor anything along the path to it. The second option finds an invigorated explorer doing everything it takes to get there. Same person in both scenarios. The nature of the task didn't change, but rather the perception that it was worth it.

The first mechanism (water on the horizon) can be to pause from reading for a few minutes to complete the *kindling questions* found in Figure 16 — prompting an initial experience with Shaper.

Revisiting Chapter 8 may also be helpful when considering these questions.

KINDLING QUESTIONS

QUESTION?	EVIDENCE (Evidence that this state was correctly identified)	IMPACT STRATEGY (Primary need & impact approach)	OBSERVED OUTCOME
What is your primary engagement state this week? *Indifferent* *Interested* *Invested*			
			CONGRUENCE? Congruence achieved? If so, document how. If not, document why.
Think of a recent, important interaction with someone you know. What was his/her engagement sate? *Indifferent* *Interested* *Invested*			
			CONGRUENCE? How to improve congruence going forward?

Figure 16

While the Shaper cycle and its related approach are universal, positive mechanisms to support its use are most powerful when they're unique to their authors.

At the organizational level, one example is to build effective Shaper into key performance indicators and reviews. More concretely, display of the invested mindset can be encouraged by personalizing a version of the *Your Impact* rule. Every employee is given two charges and the creative freedom to take them where they will. The first is to develop one idea that effectively improves the impact of the role the employee holds in the organization and how that improvement impacts related roles. The second is to consider one way the organization can deepen existing or create a new market advantage and describe what it would take to implement the idea. The ideas are presented at the time of their review or another venue, as appropriate.

While not time consuming, the mechanism of a direct, quality-driven report-out sets into motion a series of important events. To be done well, this will require further cultivating the invested mindset. At minimum, employees will spend more time in the invested state than in the indifferent or interested states. Equally important, the odds increase of great ideas with real impact flowing through the organization.

Another example is to embed the states of engagement into the organization's vocabulary. Because each state is grounded in concrete, related indicators the words *indifferent, interested,* and *invested* take on more relevant insight. When asking yourself, "where am I?" or asking the same of others the use of one of those four words triggers wonderfully rich information about its meaning and how to effectively impact it.

At the personal level, like the strategist armed with a sophisticated framework but needing to refine its use, repetition is helpful. Mechanisms that encourage consistent use are beneficial. Frequently assess your own engagement state. Get comfortable with highlighting the states' primary needs. Use the appropriate impact strategies to self-elevate. Do this with others around you. Perhaps even more powerfully, teach others to do the same — offering yourself as their first assessment case.

The statement *value is in the observance, not the occurrence* takes on more profound meaning when viewed through the lens of application. Mindset is part of the human experience and cannot be avoided. But it can be affected — often dramatically. Shaper patterns are readily understandable and repeatable. Employed well they are both enduring and dynamic; they don't go out of style and they're the cornerstone to improving any situation. Positive mechanisms along the way are helpful for building Shaper muscle memory and refining its use.

Doing this well cannot be overstated. Outcomes depend on it.

DINNER

The 1938 World Series could have been yesterday to John (name changed). It was a special moment in time, one that marked two distinct eras to his life. He was approaching twenty years old and traveled to watch one of his favorite team's, the Chicago Cubs, compete for the title. Even in his late nineties he could describe the sights and sounds and smells of sitting in Wrigley Field. They lost the series and wouldn't go on to win the title for another seventy-eight (78) years, but John loved being there.

Soon after the series closed, he shipped off to war where he was assigned to serve as a Mess Sergeant (cook) to officers and new recruits.

While war can be taxing for all, some emerge as character heroes studied across generations for their exploits. John didn't fire a shot or command a single man in battle. But he had a profound impact on those around him.

After his first assignment, in which he figured out how to feed large groups of men from a wood fire stove, he was transferred to France where he cooked for companies in Marseilles and Lyon. He traveled from point to point as needed in a baggage car — setting up his provisions at each stop. One location included the Battle of the Bulge. Without fanfare John treated each day's effort as essential to the war's outcome.

One of his proudest moments was successfully cooking 215 turkeys on the last Thanksgiving Day thousands of new recruits would experience before stepping into the bitterness of direct combat.

> "It was a great meal for those boys — it was the least I could do," is how he described the event.

In what many consider menial, John discovered something profound. Cooking fresh turkeys of that magnitude in one day had never been done before. But he didn't think anything less would do. It was a challenge he accepted because he knew what it would mean. He wasn't carelessly throwing calories at fated men. He was filling them with thoughts of belief and comradery — essential to the conviction they'd need for the mission that awaited them. John's genius wasn't that he served a lot of people dinner. It was that he served that dinner, in that way, on that day to convey just what the men needed to feel. In his own way in that ripple of time, when so many before him had taken the lesser path, he produced the innovative.

John did not go on to great fame or fortune. He did, however, live to see the Cubs successfully win the pennant in 2016. Within those bookend World Series events, he married the love of his life and adored her for 63 years before her passing. He cared deeply for his children and then grandchildren. He worked in a meatpacking plant, ran a post office, and served tirelessly in community affairs. We couldn't find a single person who had worked with or knew John who didn't describe him as constantly trying to make the people and things around him better.

John's narrative is exceptional because he was invested even in the common. He chose valuable initiative over complacent task completion. His story is a reminder that treatment of everyday scenarios largely determines the trajectory of grander designs. There's an element of John's experience in all of us. From stay-at-home parent to Fortune 500 CEO, teenager to leader of a nation, the principles hold. Dinner with John isn't about a meal at all. It's a mechanism, a symbol, a call to action. It's a mental note that mindset is the gateway to unlocking the best in any situation.

CONCLUSION

The value of something is found in its doing.

Outcomes in the human experience, good and bad, trace their roots to mindset and the positive or negative effect it unleashes. These patterns of thought directly impact engagement, which is a leading indicator of action quality, which influences results. Because mindset is not a static state, but rather fluid and capable of changing, effective shaping is key to most conceivable performance metrics.

Awareness, persistence, creativity, quality, and productivity (among others) all share roots in this process.

Embraced efficiently, Shaping is a high-impact, low-dependency investment. Required resources already exist and only need arranging. Its capacity to systematically influence outcomes cannot be overstated. While social facilitation and genetics play a role, among the many values of Shaper is its capacity for self-direction.

Consider the ability of the human body to physically self-mend. Modern medicine's primary task is to align this potential and then monitor its progress. Sutures have a part in closing a gash, but they don't really heal the wound. They strategically place the body in a position to activate its unique capabilities. The physical body functioning as it should mobilize these instincts almost immediately upon detecting the need.

Cognitive and social science highlight that a similar interaction is available through mindset patterns and the effects they trigger — with the caveat that they must be positioned to have the expected output. But unlike the physical body, which largely takes a reactive posture before moving to action, mindset can be a predictive experience (capable of influence in addition to response); it is adept at molding intended outcomes in positive ways.

Understood this way, the common path of deterministic and circumstantial explanations give way to richer appreciation for agency and self-direction. External forces make room for internal approaches. The result is the capacity for anyone with proper proficiency to shape efforts in predictable ways.

Right now. Right where you are.

Like a transcendent event that is not easily forgotten, effectively embracing the Shaper cycle (and encouraging others to do the same) can have a lasting impact.

The call to *think about what you think about* is much more than a clever grouping of words. It's largely the difference between maximized and unrealized potential.

DISCOVERY SECTION

What are your overall impressions of ways you can employ Shaper to enhance your personal development? Use the box below to write a personal "Because-I will" for an area important to you.

TEAM FOCUSED **EXERCISES**

DISCOVERY SECTION

Consider the Shaper principles applied to interpersonal dynamics. How could you help your team to fully embrace the power of Shaper? What do you anticipate this could do for your team's culture? Overall performance?

DISCOVERY SECTION

"The value of something is found in its doing." Describe at least three Shaper strengths your team exhibits (this can also be done for each individual team member). Then describe three areas for Shaper growth. How could reinforcing the former and further developing the latter benefit your team?

DISCOVERY SECTION

TEAM APPLICATION:

What are your overall impressions of ways your team can employ Shaper to enhance its mental performance and related outcomes? Use the space below to write a team focused "Because-We will" for a current or near future initiative you believe to be key to your success.

DISCOVERY SECTION

EPILOGUE

Development is as personal as it is vital. Rather than relying on others to write your epilogue – your new mental contract, take the next few lines to write your own. What mental breakthroughs have you experienced for engaging *Shaper*?

What will you now do better? Revisit this as needed to track ongoing development.

NOTES

CHAPTER ONE: THE POWER OF MINDSET

Mui, C. (2001, November 15). Innovators Beware: The Danger of Viewing Steve Jobs as a 'Tweaker'. Forbes.com.

Isaacson, W. (2011) Steve Jobs, Simon & Schuster, pp. 567 – 570.

Huntsinger, J. R., Isbell, L. M., & Clore, G. L. (2014). The affective control of thought: Malleable, not fixed, Psychological review, 121(4), 600.

Taylor, S. E., & Gollwitzer, P. M. (1995). Effects of mindset on positive illusions. Journal of personality and social psychology, 69(2), 213.

Fiske, S. T., & Taylor, S. E. (2013) Social cognition: From brains to culture. Sage.

Janis, I. L. (2008). Groupthink. IEEE Engineering Management Review, 36(1), 36.

Heckhausen, J., & Heckhausen, H. (Eds.). (2008). Motivation and action (Vol. 22). New York: Cambridge University Press.

Clark, R. D., & Word, L. E. (1972). Why don't bystanders help? Because of ambiguity? Journal of Personality and Social Psychology, 24(3), 392.

CHAPTER TWO: BEGIN WITHIN

DiMaggio, P., & Powell, W. W. (1983). The iron cage revisited: Collective rationality and institutional isomorphism in organizational fields. ASR, 48(2), 147-60.

Weber, M. (1946 [1922]). Class, status, party. In Gerth, H.H. and Wright Mills, C. (Eds). From Max Weber essays in sociology (180- 195). New York: Oxford University Press, pp. 180-195.

Singelis, T. M. (1994). The measurement of independent and inter dependent self-construal's. Personality and Social Psychology Bulletin, 20(5), 580-591.

Lee, K., & Pennings, J. M. (2002). Mimicry and the market: Adoption of a new organizational form, Academy of Management Journal, 45(1), 144-162.

Grey, C. (2004). 'Reinventing business schools: the contribution of critical management education', Academy of Management Learning and Education, 3, pp. 178–186.

Kim, W. C., & Mauborgne, R. (2004). Blue ocean strategy. If you read nothing else on strategy, read these best-selling articles., 71.

Wilson, D., & McKiernan, P. (2011). Global mimicry: Putting strategic choice back on the business school agenda. British Journal of Management, 22(3), 457-469.

"Mind–set." Merriam-Webster.com. Merriam Webster n.d. Web. August 1, 2015.

Dweck, C.S. (2006). Mindset: The new psychology of success. New York, NY, US: Random House.

Frankl, V.E. (2006). Man's search for meaning. Boston: Beacon Press. http://quickfacts.census.gov/qfd/ states/06/0615044.html. Retrieved December 30, 2015.

https://www.youtube.com/watch?v=3K_4LfzKPko. Retrieved November 23, 2015.

Singelis, T. M. (1994). The measurement of independent and inter-dependent self construals Personality and Social Psychology Bulletin, 20(5), 580-591.

Bouchard, T. J. and McGue, M. (2003), Genetic and environ-mental influences on human psychological differences. J. Neurobiol.,54: 4–45. doi: 10.1002/neu.10160

Yeager, D. S. & Dweck, C. S. (2012). Mindsets That Promote

Resilience: When Students Believe That Personal Characteristics

Can Be Developed. Educational Psychologist, 47(4), 302–314.

CHAPTER THREE: BETTER IS THE AIM

Beck, R. and Harter, J. (2015). Managers Account for 70% of Variance in Employee Engagement.

Gallup Business Journal. Retrieved July 8, 2015.

LeDoux, J. E. (2014). Coming to terms with fear. Proceedings of the National Academy of Sciences 111 (8),2871-2878.

Lieberman, M. D. (2007). Social cognitive neuro-science: a review of core processes. Annu. Rev. Psychol., 58, 259 -289.

Davidson, R. J. (2002). Anxiety and affective style: role of prefrontal cortex and amygdala. Biological psychiatry, 51(1), 68-80.

Fiske, S. T., & Taylor, S. E. (2013). Social cognition: From brains to culture. Sage. 152 – 171.

Charon, Joel M. (2004). Symbolic Interactionism An Introduction, An Interpretation, An Integration. Boston: Pearson. p. 31

Blumer, H. (1969) Symbolic Interactionism; Perspective and Method. Englewood Cliffs, NJ: Prentice-Hall

Mead, G. H. (1934). Mind, self and society (Vol. 111). University of Chicago Press.: Chicago.

Davis, R. L., & Zhong, Y. (2017). The biology of forgetting—a perspective. Neuron, 95(3), 490-503.

Richards, B. A., & Frankland, P. W. (2017). The persistence and transience of memory. Neuron, 94(6), 1071-1084.

Sachser, R. M., Haubrich, J., Lunardi, P. S., & de Oliveira Alvares, L. (2017). Forgetting of what was once learned: ExpLizng the role of postsynaptic ionotropic glutamate receptors on memory formation, maintenance, & decay. Neuropharmacology, 112 94-103.

Hadziselimovic, N., Vukojevic, V., Peter, F., Milnik, A., Fastenrath, M., Fenyves, B. G., & Papassotiropoulos,

A.(2014) Forgetting is regulated via Musashi-mediated translational control of the Arp2/3 complex. Cell,156(6), 1153-1166.

McGaugh, J. L. (2000). Memory—a century of consolidation. Science,287(5451), 248-251.

**CHAPTER FOUR:
THE SHAPER CYCLE**

"U.S. men set world record in 400 free relays." NBC News. 10 August 2008 Retrieved August 3, 2015.

Carter, C. (2009, 2014) http://greatergood.berkeley.edu/raising_happiness/post/fake_it_till_you_make_it. Retrieved September 2, 2015.

http://www.glamour.com/inspired/2015/12/lindsey-stirling-highest-earning-female-youtuber. Retrieved December 9, 2015.

Jenkins, A. C., Dodell-Feder, D., Saxe, R., & Knobe, J. (2014). The Neural Bases of Directed and Spontaneous Mental State Attributions to Group Agents. PloS one, 9(8), e105341.

Saxe, R., & Young, L. (2013). Theory of Mind: How brains think about thoughts. The handbook of cognitive neuroscience, 204-213.

Bernhardt, B. C., & Singer, T. (2012). The neural basis of empathy. Neuroscience, 35(1), 1.

Saarela, M. V., Hlushchuk, Y., Williams, A. C. D. C., Schürmann, M., Kalso, E., & Hari, R. (2007). The compassionate brain: humans detect intensity of pain from another's face. Cerebral cortex, 17(1), 230-237.

Todd, R. M., Talmi, D., Schmitz, T. W., Susskind, J., & Anderson, A. K. (2012). Psychophysical and neural evidence for emotion- enhanced perceptual vividness. The Journal of Neuro-science, ,32(33), 11201-11212

https://www.youtube.com/watch?v=A1ussHesFgs. Retrieved 1 August 2015.

http://www.newyorker.com/tech/elements/how-facebook-makes-us-unhappy. Retrieved 5 September 2015.

Lewis, C. S. (1947). The Abolition of Man.

Chamine, S. (2012). Positive intelligence: Why only 20% of teams and individuals achieve their true potential and how you can achieve yours. Greenleaf Book Group.

**CHAPTER FIVE:
THREE LEVELS OF ENGAGEMENT**

Fennell, J. (2011). Combat and morale in the North African campaign: The Eighth Army and the path to El Alamein. Cambridge University Press.

http://www.wjinst.com/wjinst/bios/leadmont.htm.Retrieved 22 December 2015.

Adair, J. (2010). Strategic leadership: How to think and plan strategically and provide direction. Kogan Page Publishers.

Fennell, J. (2011). Combat and morale in the North African campaign: The Eighth Army and the path to El Alamein. Cambridge University Press.

Beck, R. and Harter, J. (2015). Managers Account for 70% of Variance in Employee Engagement. Gallup Business Journal. Retrieved 8 July 2015.

CHAPTER SIX:
CROSS THE EXPECTATION GAP

Lagi, M., Bertrand, K. Z., & Bar-Yam, Y. (2011). The food crises and political instability in North Africa and the Middle East. Available at SSRN 1910031.

Otto, A. R., Fleming, S. M., & Glimcher, P. W. (2016). Unexpected but incidental positive outcomes predict real-world gambling. Psychological science, 0956797615618366.

Bowden, J. L., Gabbott, M., & Naumann, K. (2015). Service relationships and the customer disengagement-engagement conundrum. Journal of Marketing Management, 31(7-8),774-806.

Deutschman, A. (2001). The second coming of Steve Jobs. Currency.

Blumenthal, K. (2012). Steve Jobs: The man who thought different. Macmillan.

Slater, R. (1999). Saving big blue: Leadership lessons and turnaround tactics of IBM's Lou Gerstner. McGraw-Hill School Education Group.

Balgobin, R., & Pandit, N. (2001). Stages in the turnaround process: The Case of IBM UK. European Management Journal, 19(3), 301-316.

Gerstner, L. V. (2002). Who says elephants can't dance? inside IBM's historic turnaround. HarperCollins Publishers.

Nurse, K., Stephenson, S., & Mendez, A. (2017). Tourism, trade in services and global value chains. Future fragmentation processes: Effectively engaging with the ascendancy of global value chains, 135-156.

Chuang, H. J. (2019). Starbucks in the World. HOLISTICA–Journal of Business and Public Administration, 10(3), 99-110.

Rothaermel, F. T. (2017). Starbucks Corporation. McGraw Hill Education.

Voigt, K. I., Buliga, O., & Michl, K. (2017). Globalizing Coffee Culture: The Case of Starbucks. In Business Model Pioneers (pp. 41-53). Springer, Cham.

Moss Kanter, R. (2012). The business ecosystem: A country can become com-placent about its assets. The Harvard Magazine.

Sullivan, G. (2015). Interested care and the quality gap. Psychiatric Services.

Siegel, R. L., Miller, K. D., & Jemal, A. (2015). Cancer statistics, 2015. CA: a cancer journal for clinicians, 65(1), 5-29.

Emerson, R. M. (1976). Social exchange theory. Annual review of sociology, 335-362.

Wayne, S. J., Shore, L. M., & Liden, R. C. (1997). Perceived organizational support and leader-member exchange: A social exchange perspective. Academy of Management journal, 40(1), 82-111.

Sanfey, A. G. (2007). Social decision- making: insights from game theory and neuroscience. Science, 318(5850), 598-602.

Gergen, K. (Ed.). (2012). Social exchange: Advances in theory and research. Springer Science & Business Media.

Cook, K. S., Cheshire, C., Rice, E. R., & Nakagawa, S. (2013). Social exchange theory. In Handbook of social psychology pp. 61-88). Springer Netherlands.

Aryee, S., Walumbwa, F. O., Mondejar, R., & Chu, C. W. (2015). Accounting for the influence of overall justice on job performance: Integrating self-determination and social exchange theories. Journal of Management Studies,52(2), 231-252.

CHAPTER SEVEN: TWO FEET

Garthwaite, C., Busse, M., Brown, J., & Merkley, G. (2017). Starbucks: A story of growth. Kellogg School of Management Cases.

Schultz, H. (2012). Pour your heart into it: How Starbucks built a company one cup at a time. Hachette UK.

Koehn, N. F. (2001). Howard Schultz and Starbucks coffee company.

Buxton, L. (2017). Ditching deficit thinking: Changing to a culture of high expectations. Issues in Educational Research, 27(2), 198.

Keefer, N. (2017). The Persistence of Deficit Thinking Among Social Studies Educators. Journal of Social Studies Education Research, 8(3), 50-75.

Seligman, M. E. (2019). Positive psychology: A personal history. Annual review of clinical psychology, 15, 1-23.

Compton, W. C., & Hoffman. (2019). Positive psychology. SAGE Publications.

Lopez, S. J., Pedrotti, J. T., & Snyder, C. R. (2018). Positive psychology: The scientific and practical explorations of human strengths. Sage Publications.

Setti, R. (2019). Professional development: Mindset: How positive thinking boosts performance. LSJ: Law Society of NSW Journal, (52), 46.

King, R. B. (2016). A fixed mindset leads to negative affect. Zeitschrift für psychologie.

Imran, H., Arif, I., Cheema, S., & Azeem, M. (2014). Relationship between job satisfaction, job performance, attitude towards work, and organizational commitment. Entrepreneurship and innovation manage-ment journal, 2(2), 135-144.

Bono, J. E., Glomb, T. M., Shen, W., Kim, E., & Koch, A. J. (2013). Building positive resources: Effects of positive events and positive reflection on work stress and health. Academy of Management Journal, 56(6), 1601-1627.

Rego, A., Sousa, F., Marques, C., & Cunha, M. P. E. (2012). Optimism predicting employees' creativity: The mediating role of positive affect and the positivity ratio. European Journal of Work and Organizational Psychology,21(2), 244-270.

Avey, J. B., Luthans, F., & Youssef, C. M. (2010). The additive value of positive psychological capital in predicting work attitudes and behaviors. Journal of Management, 36(2), 430-452.

Avey, J. B., Wernsing, T. S., & Luthans, F. (2008). Can positive employees help positive organizational change? Impact of psychological capital and emotions on relevant attitudes and behaviors. The Journal of Applied Behavioral Science, 44(1), 48-70.

Luthans, F., Avolio, B. J., Avey, J. B., & Norman, S. M. (2007). Positive psychological capital: Measurement and relationship with performance and satisfaction. Personnel psychology 60(3)541-572.

Stryker, S. (1980). Symbolic interactionism: A social structural version. Benjamin-Cummings Publishing Company.

Solomon, M. R. (1983). The role of products as social stimuli: A symbolic interactionism perspective. Journal of Consumer research, 10(3), 319-329.

Blumer, H. (1980). Mead and Blumer: The convergent methodological perspectives of social behaviorism and symbolic interactionism. American Sociological Review, 409-419.

Blumer, H. (1986). Symbolic interactionism: Perspective and method. Univ of California Press.

Joel M. Charon. (2009) Symbolic interactionism: An introduction, an interpretation, an integration. Pearson College Division.

http://agln.aspeninstitute.org/ profile/3376. Retrieved September 1, 2016.

Gray, H. (2018). Turbulence and order in economic development: Institutions and economic transformation in Tanzania and Vietnam. Oxford University Press.

Chamine, S. (2012). Positive intelligence: Why only 20% of teams and individuals achieve their true potential and how you can achieve yours. Greenleaf Book Group

Lyubomirsky, S., King, L., & Diener, E. (2005). The benefits of frequent positive affect: does happiness lead to success? Psychological bulletin,131(6), 803.

Buder, S. (1967). Pullman: an experiment in industrial order and community planning, 1880-1930. Oxford University Press.

Smith, C. (2007). Urban disorder and the shape of belief: the great Chicago fire, the Haymarket bomb, and the model town of Pullman. University of Chicago Press.

Klepper, Michael; Gunther, Michael (1996), The Wealthy 100: From Benjamin Franklin to John Gates—A Ranking of the Richest Americans, Past and Present,Secaucus,New Jersey: Carol Publishing Group.

http://www.deseretnews.com/article/865648863/QA-with-Ty-Detmer-Talking-about-the-past-present-and-future-of-BYU- football.html?pg=all. Retrieved March 1, 2016.

www.gastroenophile.com/013/03/interview-with-perus-gaston- acurio-by.html Retrieved September 1, 2016.

Benkirane, O. (2019). Acting on purpose: the reflections of MIT student entrepreneurs (Doctoral dissertation, Massachusetts Institute of Technology).

Sternad, D., Kennelly, J. J., & Bradley, F. (2017). Digging deeper: How purpose-driven enterprises create real value. Routledge.

Cashman, K. (2017). Leadership from the inside out: Becoming a leader for life. Berrett-Koehler Publishers.

Creswell, JD. (2017). Mindfulness interventions. Annual review of psychology, 68, 491-516.

CHAPTER EIGHT: BUILD CONGRUENCE

Ajzen, I., & Fishbein, M. (1980). Understanding attitudes and predicting social behaviour.

Ajzen, I. (1991). The theory of planned behavior. Organizational behavior and human decision processes, 50(2), 179-211.

Bandura, A. (1991). Social cognitive theory of self-regulation. Organizational behavior and human decision processes, 50(2), 248-287.

Conner, M., & Armitage, C. J. (1998). Extending the theory of planned behavior: A review and avenues for further research. Journal of appli-ed social psychology, 28 (15), 1429-1464.

Hofmann, W., Schmeichel, B. J., & Baddeley, A. D. (2012). Executive functions and self-regulation. Trends in cognitive sciences, 16(3), 174-180.

Burnette, J. L., O'Boyle, E. H., VanEpps, E. M., Pollack, J. M., & Finkel, E. J. (2013). Mindsets matter: A meta-analytic review of implicit theories and selfregulation Psychological Bulletin, 139(3), 655.

Festinger, L. (1962). A theory of cognitive dissonance (Vol. 2). Stanford University press.

Elliot, A. J., & Devine, P. G. (1994). On the motivational nature of cognitive dissonance: Dissonance as psychological discomfort. Journal of personality and social psychology, 67(3), 382.

Harmon-Jones, E., Harmon-Jones, C., & Levy, N. (2015). An action-based model of cognitive-dissonance processes. Current Directions in Psychological Science, 24(3), 184-189.

Hinojosa, A. S., Gardner, W. L., Walker, H. J., Cogliser, C., & Gullifor, D. (2016). A Review of Cognitive Dissonance Theory in Management Research. Journal of Management.

CHAPTER NINE: REINFORCE YOUR AGENCY

Grove, Andrew S. Swimming Across: a Memoir, Hachette Book Group (2001) Prologue

Isaacson, Walter (1997-12-29). "TIME: Man Of The Year" Time.

"Former Intel chief Andrew Grove dies aged 79", BBC, March 22, 2016

"Andy Grove, Valley Veteran Who Founded Intel, Dies at 79", Bloomberg, March 21, 2016.

Gaither, Chris (2001-11-12). "Andy Grove's Tale of His Boyhood in Wartime". The New York Times. Retrieved September 04, 2016. newsroom.intel.com/ news-releases/andrew-s-grove-1936-2016/. Retrieved September04, 2016.

www.fiercebiotech.com/medical-devices/stryker-ceo-touts- paradigm-shift Retrieved October 1, 2016.

phx.corporateir.net/phoenix.zhtml?c=118965&p=irol-newsArticle&ID=2139404.

Retrieved September 3, 2016 careers.stryker.com/assets/en-us/pdfs/SYK-factsheet-April-2015.pdf Retrieved October 12, 2016.www.bloomberg.com/ features/2016-satya-nadella-interview-issue/ Retrieved September 6, 2016.

Emerson, W. (1929) Blight. The Complete Writings of Ralph. Waldo Emerson, New York: Wm. H Wise & Co. 874.

White, C. (2003) The Life and Times of Little Richard, United Kingdom: Omnibus Press; 3rd edition.

Wilde, O. (1908). A Woman of No Importance: A Play. London: Methuen.

Wilde, O. (1914). The Soul of Man. Humphreys.

Kuhn, T. S. (2012). The structure of scientific revolutions. University of Chicago press.

CHAPTER TEN: PROVIDE EFFECTIVE FEEDBACK

Mischel, W., Ebbesen, E. B., & Raskoff Zeiss, A. (1972). Cognitive and attentional mechanisms in delay of gratification. Journal of personality and social psychology, 21(2), 204.

Kidd, C. Palmeri, H., & Aslin, R.N. (2013). Rational snacking. Young children's decision-making on the marshmallow task is moderated by beliefs about environmental reliability Cognition, 126(1) 109-114.

Mischel, W., Shoda, Y., & Rodriguez, M. L. (1989). Delay of gratification in children. Science, 244(4907)933-938.

ABOUT THE AUTHOR

B. Tom Hunsaker, PhD is an international bestselling author and trusted executive advisor. He previously served as Associate Dean of Innovation for the Thunderbird School of Global Management (then top-ranked worldwide in its field and a unit of Arizona State University, #1 in the U.S. for innovation) and helped to pioneer the Global Challenge Lab. Tom is among the very few in the institution's history to receive in each graduate-level program the distinguished teaching award given to its top professor: Executive, Full-time, and Online. He has also held leadership positions for growth firms in the performance technology and analytical sciences industries. Tom's research and publications are recommended reading in leading universities, applied by thousands of enterprises and their leaders worldwide, published in top outlets such as *Harvard Business Review* and *MIT Sloan Review* (where he co-authors the breakthrough series 'The Strategy of Change') and have been featured in popular press globally. Tom is regularly asked to advise Fortune 500 and emerging enterprise leadership teams and is a noted speaker who has delivered keynotes on four continents. He and his family enjoy serving in their community, traveling, and exploring the outdoors together.

Visit tomhunsaker.com

NEXT LEVEL IMPACT

PEOPLE THE WORLD OVER ARE RETOOLING TO MEET TODAY'S DYNAMIC DEMANDS AND SHAPE TOMORROW'S ADVANTAGES. ARE YOU?

World-class enterprises from the Fortune 500 to emerging scale ups and thousands in between have benefited from methods and insights we publish.

www.ingramcontent.com/pod-product-compliance
Lightning Source LLC
Chambersburg PA
CBHW051519230426
43668CB00012B/1663